Have Fun, Fall in Love... and Get Paid to Do It!

A GUIDE TO CAREER BLISS

ROBERT S. BURNS

PEANUT BUTTER
PUBLISHING

Seattle, Washington
Portland, Oregon
Denver, Colorado
Vancouver, B.C.

Library of Congress No. 96-067552

Robert S. Burns

Have Fun, Fall in Love ... and Get Paid to Do It!

ISBN 0-89716-616-7

11.0026

Editing & Production: Susi Henderson

First printing February 1996

10 9 8 7 6 5 4 3 2 1

PEANUT BUTTER PUBLISHING

226 2nd Avenue West • Seattle, WA 98119 • 206-281-5965

Old Post Office Bldg. • 510 S.W. 3rd • Portland, OR 97201 • 503-222-5527

Cherry Creek • 50 S. Steele • Suite 850 • Denver, CO 80209 • 303-322-0065

Suite 230 – 1333 Johnston Street • Pier 32, Granville Island

• Vancouver, B.C. V6H 3R9 • 604-688-0320 •

e mail: pnutpub@aol.com

Internet: http://www.pbpublishing.com

Printed in Canada

Table of Contents

1. You Call This Fun? 9

2. Stop Whining and Get Your Job
   Working for *You!* 19

3. Creativity at Work 33

4. Power to the Communicators 45

5. Image Building 59

6. Working at Networking 69

7. Nice Guys Finish 83

8. Erogenous Zones 91

9. Climbing the Mountain 103

10. Unorthodox Wins the Race 117

11. Love It or Leave It 127

12. Jobs in the Twenty-First Century 137

13. You Are What You Do 151

14. Keep On Loving Your Job 159

DEDICATION

*This book is dedicated to anyone and everyone who has
ever aspired to become greater tomorrow than they are today.*

ACKNOWLEDGMENTS

Sincere thanks to M.L. for her encouragement, support and editing. Special thanks to K.H., R.M. and to B.G. for their support of the project. Most of all, thanks to all of the great people I've worked with over the years who gave me so much to write about, especially to those who made it difficult for me, as they were the source of some of my best material.

ABOUT THE AUTHOR

Robert S. Burns is the President of Burns & Associates Consulting, providing consultation to businesses and corporations, primarily to private vocational schools and institutions. Previously, as one of the directors of a leading private vocational college, he spent eight years developing career strategies for thousands of students. He was instrumental in building a small franchise school into the largest private vocational school in British Columbia.

Mr. Burns is currently the President of the Private Career Training Association, representing over 140 private vocational schools throughout British Columbia. He is the Vice Chair of the Education Reference Group for the British Columbia Labour Force Development Board and Board Member and Treasurer of the Pacific Association for Continuing Education.

In addition to his consulting practise, Mr. Burns remains active as a performing musician, playing engagements throughout the Pacific Northwest. Publishers include Chappell Canada, Almo Irving (A&M Records) and Arista Publishing.

INTRODUCTION

If you can develop a lasting love for your job and have fun doing it, you will have found one of the keys to happiness. Sigmund Freud said that work is mankind's closest link to reality. If this is the case, why not make it an enjoyable reality?

Why settle for a loveless working relationship or be counted among the "working wounded"? There is more than just a place for you in the workforce. Success is out there waiting to greet you. All you have to do is reach out and embrace it.

In the following pages I offer you practical strategies on how to succeed at the most critical relationship of your life ... your job! Learn how to take control of your destiny, become empowered in today's job market and advance toward career bliss. So have fun, fall in love (with your job) ... and get paid to do it!

YOU CALL THIS FUN?

The cruel radio alarm pierces the night. It's dark and it's cold. Needing more sleep, we are once again summoned to another day of drudgery. Between the slaps to the snooze bar on the alarm, the announcer's voice jabs into our dreams with fragments of urban horror. Our fluffy thoughts are displaced by that wicked voice, and in our semiconscious state we are transported to the galley of a slave ship from one of those cheesy B movie epics. Can you see the evil taskmaster banging his drum as the slaves sit side by side rowing away? Can you feel the lash on their backs as they toil endlessly through the sweat and blood? The beer we drank before going to bed is gnawing at our bladder. The convergence of that discomfort and the 6:00 A.M. traffic report shock us upright out of our dreams and into another day of work.

Does this sound familiar? Most of us have had a version of this nightmare as we dreamed of our jobs. Is it as bad as all that? For many working people it might as well be. Of all the people working today, only a small percentage of them can honestly say they love their work.

Many of us, in fact most of us, believe that we could or should be doing something more interesting, more challenging or more rewarding. If possible, the majority of working people would alter their jobs to make their work more satisfying. We've all heard phrases like "He's just a frustrated artist," or "She sees herself as `management'," or "He's nothing but an armchair quarterback." The simple truth of the matter is that most people are unhappy with many aspects of their jobs.

With the hope of career bliss so faint for so many, it is not surprising that working society is straining at its very seams. What keeps the system from collapsing completely? What could possibly be powerful enough to drive so many of us to toil endlessly at these loveless working relationships? It's called *the rent!* That's right. The rent, the mortgage, the car payments! The children's education fund, the retirement savings plan, the food on the table, the very shirt on your back! Perhaps this *is* a bad dream come true. Are we destined to become intellectually bankrupt and emotionally numb as we are forced to slave away for those cruel taskmasters, our creditors?

The End of the Road or the Reprieve?

Has the occupational road we've chosen come to a bleak dead end? Is the carrot of carefree weekends, lazy summer holidays and the eventuality of our golden years nothing more than a sick joke? Has all our good faith only led us to a heartless deal we made with our credit cards? Never! There is hope! This is the eleventh hour call granting a reprieve from "career death row." Read on and find out why you don't have to settle for a loveless working relationship. Instead, you can learn to have more fun, develop a lasting love for your job and get paid to do it!

The Wrong Reason

Imagine the reaction of most people if they were to win the *Big Lottery*. The majority of working people would march directly up to their boss and tell him to "take your job and...!" This reaction is based on the assumption that most of us work for one main purpose, to pay the rent. So it follows that if we win the Big Lotto or Auntie croaks and leaves us a bundle, we will gain financial freedom, the payments will go away and so can the job.

How about that guy from Kalamazoo who wins ten million bucks and continues working at his old job. Is he three sheets to the wind? Is he certifiably insane? No. He has learned how to love his job. He has a different reason for working.

Instead of waiting for our numbers to come up in the Lotto or for poor Auntie to die, we need to realign our thinking and come up with a better reason for working than money. Wait a minute! This is going against just about everything we ever learned about working from the time we were old enough to have a job delivering the morning paper. The irresistible notion that a pay check and starvation are inseparable is hard to fight. But in order to achieve "career bliss" we must take that first frightening step and divorce ourselves from the idea that work equals [only] material gain.

Studies show us that of all the issues facing employees today, their level of pay is not the biggest concern. The biggest problem facing most employees is the feeling that their skills are under-utilized. The second most common problem is poor relationships with supervisors. Money is *not* the big problem.

We need another reason for working. Not just any reason, we need the *right* reason—one that will give us the attachment to our work that will go beyond dedication, beyond commitment, all the way to *ownership* of our job. Ownership that will enable us to make a *connection* between our personal needs and our professional goals—a connection that does not separate personal development from professional achievement. We must develop the type of ownership that will allow us to see ourselves as Olympic champions going for the gold in every task and assignment.

We want the kind of ownership that the heroic fire fighter shows when he runs into that burning building to save the children from impending disaster. Does he stop to think, "Am I getting paid enough to do this?" or "I'm not really having a great day so far, am I really into this?" Of course not! When the lifeguard jumps into the icy water to save the failing swimmer, does he or she stop to think about their position in the organization? Do they wait to calculate their earnings per stroke before they swim out to save the struggling swimmer? We'd better hope not!

These working individuals have made the connection to their work that is more than unshakable—they have developed a connection that is umbilical! Your own connection will come from the belief that there isn't anyone in this world more qualified to do what you are about to accomplish. And if there is, they aren't here today to do it! You are the one who has been chosen to triumph in this challenge. And in your achievement, your true reward will not come externally, from supervisors or employers, but internally, from your own sense of self accomplishment.

Powerful stuff! Before I give you a hernia from power lifting that 600-lb. weight in the 2004 Olympics, let's get back to some fundamentals that will get us on our way up to that Olympic pinnacle. Let's go back to the beginning when we established our feelings toward work and accomplishment. As a kid, do you remember having to clean up your room or mow the lawn on a hot summer day? I doubt that many of us jumped in there and immediately did these chores without any prodding from our parents.

Try to remember past the prodding and your initial resistance to the chore and get to the memory of the job being well on its way, the end clearly in sight and that great feeling you had from seeing the results of your labours. Hey, that ice cream cone or the fifty cents your Dad gave you was nice, but remember how you felt about the results? That's it! That's the reason, the ownership I am talking about.

We have to get back to that naiveté that will allow us to get in touch with the feeling of accomplishment and not just the ice cream cone or the fifty cents. It is this naiveté that produces the type of thinking that will release the shackles that are holding us to the oars of that big corporate slave ship. Within this kind of thinking lies liberation from occupational slavery and the freedom to develop the skills to further ourselves as well as our employers. This is the type of thinking that will give us ownership of our careers, our jobs, and will promote *self-empowerment*. Self-empowerment in that once we have taken ownership of our career, *we* are now in charge! No one else. Once we have made that connection, we will have a good reason for working—better yet, we will have the *right* reason.

It is my belief that all of us can make this critical connection and take ownership of our jobs. More importantly, you, the reader, are probably ready to do it now! You found this book, it did not find you. That indicates that you have been evaluating your relationship with your job. This is the beginning of a very important process, because not only are you taking the first steps toward self-empowerment and ownership of your job, you are doing it for the right reason. You are doing it for *you*. You need the right reason to be working, but it also has to be your reason, not my reason, not your spouse's reason, not your parent's or friend's reason, it must be *your* reason.

Whose Idea Is This, Anyway?

I was eighteen, just out of high school and about to experience my first full-time job. My father was a great salesman and he convinced me to "go North" and discover Canada. Although he had never done it, he thought it was a great idea for me to go up there and see the world. After all, he had gone to Istanbul, Turkey when he was my age so I could certainly go a mere 1,000 kilometres or so to seek my fortune. Of course, Turkey had the warm and romantic Mediterranean, and belly dancers fanning you with palm leaves while you were sipping your tea.

The images of those wafting palm leaves were firmly fixed in my mind on the entire flight into the Yukon. However, those images quickly faded as I stepped off the plane into a biting wind accompanied by icy, Arctic temperatures. The snow swirled around me as I ran toward the small bus that was to take me further north to the destiny my father had told me so much about. I can still remember seeing the northern lights silhouetted on that huge black sky as our bus wound its way above the cliffs of the Nahannie, also known as the Headless River. My heart sank as our driver told the story of mysterious headless bodies that had been found on its banks many years ago. Images of merciless decapitation filled my head as we ploughed along the snow packed road down the mountain into the night.

This bus made only one stop, Tungsten—the ore, the mine, the town, all one and the same. Hundreds of miles from anywhere or anyone. Total isolation. If you went out of the camp for a walk and got lost, you would freeze to death in a matter of hours. It was the end of the line. I felt fear creeping over me, but at the same time a certain excitement about facing this unknown adventure. After a couple of hours we arrived in Tungsten. I had my work clothes issued and got checked into the bunk house in boot camp fashion and got ready to start my first shift.

Because it was about 40 degrees below zero and I fully expected to face the harsh elements, I put on my long underwear before heading off to work. As soon as I got over to the mill, I got my first assignment, shovelling muck down by the furnace! It was hotter than hell down in that hole and with that long underwear on it was unbearable. I knew it was going to be embarrassing, but I was going to have to make contact with the Neanderthal overseer, the shift boss. "Excuse me, sir, but may I go down to the locker room and change my underwear?" "What?!" he replied. "Be quiet and keep shovelling that muck, you little sissy! You'll have to wait for your lunch break to do that." Talk about a slave ship! The shift finally ended, but only after I'd lost about ten pounds in perspiration.

We then marched like POWs to the cook shack and I got my first experience of living and dining with hard rock miners and labourers. This was a motley crew, a rugged mosaic of nomadic workers from all over the world. Language was crude and there was an orgy of burping and farting and hork-down dining. I felt as though this was my first day in prison amongst hardened criminals—murderers and rapists.

I was terrified, but I had to muster up the courage to ask someone to pass the salt. I managed to do that with my head low and my voice lower. The salt shaker was passed over by this meaty hand with only one finger and a thumb.

"Go ahead. Take it!" a rough voice said. I looked up and saw the twisted claw belonged to a huge man with a face that looked like someone had taken a cork screw, stuck it through his lips and started twisting! My horror was more obvious than I thought because someone said in a low voice "Don't worry son, it's only Stumpy; he's okay." Later I was told that he was just a regular miner-type-of-guy until a blasting cap went off in his hand and up into his face up at the old mine some years ago.

"Stumpy," I thought. Explosions at the mine. Wait a minute! I wanted to be a musician when I grew up. I didn't want my tender little digits working around huge pieces of unforgiving industrial machinery. I wasn't cut out for this type of work. The moment I looked down at that disfigured set of prongs, I knew that Tungsten wasn't going to be a large part of my career destiny. My father would be disappointed but as soon as my hitch was up, I would be on the first bus back to civilization.

I could tell many stories about my time up at the mine, but that will be left for another book. The important thing I want to share from that experience is that you will never be happy if you are in a job to satisfy someone else's expectations. If father, mother, spouse or friends are expecting you to work at a particular job or to be in a certain profession, that will never be the right reason to be in that job.

Remember, the only good reason you can ever have to succeed at anything must be your own reason. If you are in a job or profession to please someone else, you will find it very difficult to attain career bliss.

NOTEWORTHY SAYS:

- It's hard to have fun if your only motive for working is money

- We need to make a connection between our personal needs and our professional goals

- Self-empowerment will free you from a loveless working relationship

- The reason for being in any job or profession must be your own and no one else's

∽ **2** ∾

STOP WHINING AND GET YOUR JOB WORKING FOR *YOU!*

In the current economy there is a phrase that is being used, the "jobless recovery." This "jobless recovery" is indicative of the recent restructuring and downsizing many companies have undergone to maintain profitability in competitive global markets. What this means is that there are fewer and fewer jobs available. Furthermore, good jobs are fewer still. If current trends continue, there is little reason to believe things will improve in this area. Whatever the economic experts and labour market analysts choose to call it, the truth of the matter is that we are in the midst of an employment crisis.

How does this employment crisis affect you and your job? The most immediate impact this crisis has on us is the increased restriction of job mobility. If we don't like our job, it may not be such a good idea to jump ship in this kind of labour market. Considering that jobs are scarce and good jobs are a rarity, if you have a job with any potential, you'd better keep it!

Rather than throwing yourself into unknown waters to the mercy of sharks and other predators like your creditors, you are much better off making the most out of what you have in place. If you have been in a job for any length of time you have probably built up a number of contacts (internally and externally) and developed some relationships that have a great deal of potential.

Return on Investment

If you include preparation and commuting time to and from work, it is easy to conclude that you spend the majority of your waking hours directly or indirectly working. If you also take into account the time you spend thinking and talking about it, you will soon realize that your work consumes the largest part of your life. Why not make it one of the best parts? Okay, now you think I've sold you out. You liked the part about the cruel taskmasters etc., and now I'm going to get you to love your boss, that old sonofa..., Mr. Smith/Ms. Jones! Not quite; you're going to learn how to love your job and make it show. Then 'ol man Smith will love and appreciate you and when he does that, you might even like him, too.

The most important thing you can invest is your time. As with any investment, you want the maximum return. Not only have you invested a good deal of time into your current situation, you have your entire future to consider. So if that job and you are going to be together for a while, don't stay in the marriage just for the payments; make it a rewarding and beautiful relationship. Instead of just working for that job, why not get that job working for you?

Even if you have a lacklustre job that appears to be one-dimensional, you can do something about it. In fact, you have at least two distinct choices. You can slog away without direction at that job, or you can take the bull by the horns and attempt to gradually transform that so-so job into a good job, perhaps even a great job.

One thing that you will be required to do to transform a dead-end job into a thing of beauty that begs to be loved passionately is to change the way you think about your job. As long as you accept the idea that you are working just for that paycheck and prostituting yourself to those wicked taskmasters, the best you can hope for is to haplessly continue working at that marginal job. If you can broaden your horizon and start to think of that job as a vehicle for opportunity rather than a millstone around your neck, you can begin to get that job *working for you* instead of working for your job.

Your Job as a Vehicle for Opportunity

A vehicle for opportunity. Instead of the vehicle driving you to your grave the day after you get that retirement Timex on your 65th birthday, why not get in the driver's seat of that vehicle and wheel your way down the road to self-empowerment and success? Take that big step, assume responsibility, and take control of your own career destiny.

Although you are a team player in every respect and strive to be considered as such, your primary goal should be individual advancement. The theory being that as you advance as an individual, the organization you associate yourself with will reap the benefits of that advancement. Now you're back to a "reason" for working. It's not just the money, it's an opportunity to advance. And here's the big bonus ... you get paid to do it! The advancement is the real paycheck, the monetary reward is just a dividend.

From time to time you hear about people with these "plum" jobs, jobs where people get paid to go to school to learn something that makes them better at their job. And when they finish that training, they become more valuable to their employer and their job even gets better. Talk about win-win! Although you may not have realized it, you may already be in a job that has the potential to become one of those plum jobs. If you start thinking of your job as a vehicle for opportunity, and realize that you are actually being paid to advance yourself, your job can take on a whole new dimension.

I stated earlier that the majority of working people would alter their jobs if it was possible to do so. I would now like to reintroduce that concept but this time reword it to read: It is possible for the majority of working people to transform a mundane job into a vehicle for opportunity.

One of the main reasons employees have difficulty recognizing this opportunity is that they feel there is little or no room for advancement in their job. They are waiting for someone to create opportunity for them, looking for others to recognize their abilities and advance them. Wake up! The person who has the most control over your career advancement is YOU! Wake up and stop waiting. Instead of just sitting still and trying to outlive everybody else, take action and make something happen for yourself!

Don't TELL Me You Love Me, SHOW Me You Love Me

Just about all of us feel that we have a lot more talent to offer our job than we are called upon to provide. Let's make sure that we are prepared to take this presumption beyond the theoretical level by *demonstrating, without reservation, how much we **have** to offer.* Employers are not as interested in hearing you tell them how great you are as they are in seeing how great you are. From the employer's perspective, he or she has hired you to provide a service in exchange for the pay they give you. Two things that all employers are interested in are generating more revenue and reducing expenditures. They like this because it translates into a more profitable company. So why not find ways to improve the "service" you provide in a way that will help your employers achieve their goals and give you recognition for helping them?

Remember, You're in Charge!

When you start to look at this company as if it were your own, you may suddenly come up with all sorts of ways to streamline what you do. To reorganize, to become more efficient. Then you can start thinking about where you interact with other areas in your organization and how those interactions can be improved. You can consider generating initiatives and proposals that will increase productivity and profitability. These things will get the attention of your employer very quickly.

Wait a minute! That's not my job, it's the bosses' job to do that. Not any more. You're the boss! You are the centre of your own industry. You are an industry within an industry. Once you've rounded that corner and realized that you have the power to improve your position and have recognized this as an opportunity, you have attached *value* to your job. Once you have done this, you have made the first major step toward taking ownership of your job.

Employers cherish and "die for" employees who take ownership of their jobs. Not only are these people very much in demand, they are few and far between. Although there is a great deal of competition for jobs today, there is nowhere near the same level of competition by employees to take ownership of their jobs. This presents an excellent opportunity for those who are prepared to work toward obtaining that ownership.

Self-Evaluation

To get a direction established for ourselves in our job, we need to examine what it is that we are hoping to achieve and how we are going to go about achieving it. Let's start by trying to determine exactly how *ready* we are to make something happen with our job. Considering how much our job dominates our time, we have to realize that what we are really talking about is changing our life. This level of readiness sounds like it will be very difficult to determine but it doesn't have to be. How ready a person is to make a life change can usually be measured by exactly how long they are committed to following through with that change.

That commitment can be generated by a number of reasons like; "If things don't improve in my job I am going to quit" or "I refuse to continue without more of a challenge" or "I have made a promise to myself to advance my career this year, no matter what." Again, by virtue of the fact that you are examining this book and perhaps other books of this nature, you may be ready now.

Let's continue by doing an *attitude check*. We all assume that we have a great attitude towards things, but do we really? Try to be objective here and see how you feel about some of the following:

Attitude Check	*Good*	*Bad*
Your supervisors	❏	❏
The pay you receive for your work	❏	❏

People in your organization who receive   ❏   ❏
    more pay than you do

The products you produce   ❏   ❏

The service you offer   ❏   ❏

Your opportunity for advancement   ❏   ❏

The hours you work   ❏   ❏

If you have negative feelings about any of the above, maybe your attitude isn't as great as you think it is. You need to improve this before you continue. One thing you can do to improve your attitude is try to come to terms with your position in the organization. Although you may not be exactly where you want to be at the moment, where you are today is only going to be a springboard to bigger and better things. Remember, where you are today is not as important as where you can be tomorrow. After applying some of the ideas in this book, you are going to make some fundamental changes in the way you think about your job and when you do, you can begin your ascent toward career bliss.

Now make a "Wish List" of what you would like to receive from your job.

Here are some examples:

Promotion: Opportunity for vertical movement within the organization

Advancement: Possible to evolve both professionally and personally

Recognition: Acknowledgment of abilities by supervisors and coworkers

Respect: Desire for ideas and efforts to be embraced

Prestige: Acknowledgment of advancement

Further Training: Professional development supported by organization

More Challenge: Responsibility increased as ability is demonstrated

Better Utilization of Skills: Opportunity to exercise individuality and apply unique skills

Create your own "Wish List" here:

Promotion:

Advancement:

Recognition:

Respect:

Prestige:

Further Training:

More Challenge:

Better Utilization of Skills:

Now make a list of things that you are prepared to give *to* your job.

Some Possible Examples:

Commitment: Put the needs of the organization and its customers ahead of your own

Time: Give extra time to follow tasks through to satisfactory conclusions

Ideas: Anticipate problems and develop ways to avoid them, don't just correct them

Focused Effort: Be able to maintain objectives despite distractions

Positive Attitude: Maintain optimism and confidence in your ability to provide solutions

Areas In Which You Will Give:

Commitment:

Time:

Ideas:

Focused Effort:

Positive Attitude:

Try to balance the points on one list with the other so that you are as equally prepared to give to your job as you are to receive from it.

Job Evaluation

Now that we're ready to take a new approach to our work, let's do an evaluation and see what kind of hidden potential our job has. Let's begin by making a list of all the positive things that we can think of about our job—the obvious things that make it tolerable, even enjoyable. Then arrange them in the order of most to least important. (If you can't think of one positive thing about your job, put this book down immediately and start looking for another job!)

If you can come up with even a few things on your list, let's expand the search by looking more closely at some of the possible assets we may have overlooked. Make sure you leave no stone unturned because you probably have a lot more to work with than you think you do.

Possible Assets in Our Job:

- ❑ Relationships with coworkers
- ❑ Opportunity to develop interpersonal skills
- ❑ Potential to advance listening skills
- ❑ Access to and association with management
- ❑ Ability to make new contacts through work
- ❑ Training available
- ❑ Potential to observe and learn from others
- ❑ Opportunity for self-improvement

- ❑ Producing useful product(s)
- ❑ Location of work
- ❑ _____
- ❑ _____
- ❑ _____

The deeper we go into the possibilities and potential our job has, we will discover a lot of positive aspects to it. In fact, the more objective we become about our job, the more likely we are to turn up hidden potential. One way to become more objective is to think of someone you know who has what you feel is the "ultimate" job. Find out everything you can about that person's job and do an analysis of what makes that job so great. Try not to pay attention to the power, the hours of work or the monetary aspects of that job, try to locate the substance of what makes it such a good job.

Then compare it to your job and closely examine the differences no matter how vast they seem. Don't focus on how different the jobs are, focus on why they are different. How did he get into that job? What mechanisms were in place to facilitate her promotion and what part of that process can be applied to our own situation? Ignore the obvious reasons, like being related to the owner of the company, etc. Look at the accessible things their job has that our job does not. How can we structure our position so that we can put some of the same mechanics in place that worked so well for the person in that ultimate job.

Let's take the smallest things, the little steps, and use them to become the first rungs of our *ladder to career bliss.* The bottom of the ladder, the foundation, was established when we started to change the way we think about our job. Some of the next rungs fell into place as a result of our evaluation of ourselves and our work. We can build more rungs onto our ladder with ideas we gain from the comparison between our job and that ultimate job. Still other rungs may come from further training, and by finding ways to apply more of our skills to our job. The more we reexamine our position, the more responsible we become for our job. As we become more responsible, the application of more of our skills will become possible.

NOTEWORTHY SAYS:

- Get your job working for you
- Your job is a vehicle for opportunity
- When you attach Value to your work, you take ownership of your job
- Do a thorough evaluation of yourself and your job

Realizing career bliss is like climbing a ladder.

Take it one step at a time.

∞ 3 ∞

CREATIVITY AT WORK

One of the biggest complaints I hear, time and time again, is that people feel there is little or no room for creativity in their job. This may appear to be the case on the surface, but if we dig a little deeper, we will find that there is a lot more potential for creativity in our work than we ever imagined.

There is a very common misconception that because our particular job involves repetition, it is boring or pointless and that creativity cannot be applied to it. This line of reasoning is not only counterproductive to our career success, it will only serve to cloud our vision and keep us from seeing the wealth of amazing opportunities we have to be creative at work.

Some people would have us believe that creativity is something that we are born with, like a natural ability to play the piano or to paint pictures. I strongly disagree with this notion; I believe that everyone has the ability to be creative. It may be true that some people are naturally more creative than others, but all of us have the potential to develop our level and scope of creativity. This is due to the fact that creativity is not just a God-given talent, it can be developed just like the many other skills we use every day.

In order to become more creative at work or in any other situation, the first thing we must do is become aware of the *creative process*. We must acknowledge and accept this creative process. In an effort to understand the creative process, let's sit back, relax, open our minds and pretend to go back in history.

Let's go back past the industrial revolution, past the Renaissance period, let's go way back past the ancient Roman times all the way back to the prehistoric age of the Cave People. Let's imagine that we are way back in time and we are going to observe the birth of one of the first great creative ideas in history.

Og and Grog

Back in the time of the Cave People, there were two guys named Og and Grog. One day, Og and Grog wandered away from their village and came to a clearing on the edge of a forest. The two Cave People sat there on a log, naked, with no technology to protect them.

Suddenly, out of the forest jumped a hungry pack of wolves, ready for their lunch! Terrified, Og and Grog ran away with the wolves pursuing them. They ran down a path that led to an old river bed with rocks and dry bushes everywhere. In an effort to frighten off the pursuing wolves, Og picked up a rock and began beating it against another rock. As Og beat one rock against the other, sparks began to fly everywhere. As the sparks flew, they landed on a bush nearby and the dry bush suddenly burst into flames!

Og was terrified by this event. As he saw the hungry wolves bearing down on Grog and himself, he quickly deduced that because he was afraid of this flaming phenomena, these aggressive, hairy creatures just might be too. Og bravely grabbed the burning bush, pulled it out of the ground and held it out at the wolves.

The wolves howled with fright and ran away! Og saved Grog and himself and in the process discovered fire! Even though he did not understand it, Og had made a great discovery by utilizing the *creative process.*

Most great ideas are born out of other ideas, just like in the story of the Cave People. By connecting familiar ideas in a new sequence or presenting ideas in a different context, we can create the spark that will ignite the flames of a totally new idea! We link one idea to the next until something brilliant, something inspirational evolves out of the creative process.

Even with the dullest task facing us, we can generate creativity by changing the sequence of the chores or by examining the work in a different context. This involves taking risks at times. Risks in wandering off the beaten path of our routine and trying to approach those old obstacles from new directions. The creative process has a much better chance of occurring if we are prepared to take risks to stimulate the process.

In my career as a musician, I had many jobs where I had to play the same songs over and over. In order to stimulate the creative process, I would take risks with my performance and insert a different chord or a new phrase into the sequence of information (the song) and suddenly creativity was generated by this new approach to my performance. This same principle can be applied to repetitive aspects of many jobs and can yield some amazing results.

Take risks in your job. You too can access the creative process; it's out there waiting for you, right behind the familiar landmarks on that well-travelled trail. Go ahead, take a chance; if you don't try, you will never know how much fun your job can be.

Peasants or Performers?

Not only can we all be creative, whether we know it or not, we are all performers in our own right. From the diva singing "The Marriage of Figaro" to the support worker in the office, we are all performers. Each of us is paid to do a task and to produce a performance of one kind or another. Each of us is in a position to apply creativity to our performance.

We are not alone in our challenge to cope with repetition in our work. In our quest to sustain inspiration in our assignments we have something in common with some of the most glamorous, the most successful and the highest paid people working today! In the performing arts—in theatre, for example—there are people who perform the same show, repeat the same task six nights a week with matinees on Saturdays and Sundays. The same script, the same routine for weeks, months, even years on end.

There have been shows like "Cats," or "The King and I," that have had decades of performances. They've had to bury people and replace them with new players before the show ended its run! Not only do these great performers repeat the same task night after night for months and years on end, they consistently aspire to give powerful performances every time!

When we are faced with that repetitive chore, let's stop for one moment and identify with these great performers. By identifying, we can develop the focus we require to complete the task. We can empower ourselves to put our heart and soul into the delivery of our performance. No matter how simple the job, we are not peasants, we are truly performers and we are not alone.

Taking our Performance Over the Top

Now that we have made the link between ourselves and performers, we can start to think about ways to take our performance over the top just like those accomplished performers do. Once we put ourselves in the same realm as the great performers, we can't settle for anything less than taking *our* performance over the top. For more ideas on how to connect with the drive and commitment of performers, I encourage you to see any performance of a national theatrical production or major arena musical group that comes to your city. Observe the passion these performers pour into their jobs. They are excellent examples of people who love their work. These people will not only entertain you, they are sure to inspire you as well.

The Catalyst

Just like any creative performer, we require a catalyst to stimulate our creativity—the pack of wolves chasing us, forcing us to be innovative—the element that will push us into uncharted territories. Where on earth will we locate this catalyst? It's not as mysterious as it sounds. It's usually right in front of us. It can be our customers, our coworkers, maybe even our boss. The catalyst is wherever we can find it!

If your job puts you into contact with the public, then the catalyst is easily located. It's the people—the fascinating, dynamic collage of humanity that faces us every day. When people come in contact with other people in a commercial situation, they tend to have many expectations regarding the outcome. This presents a great opportunity for us if we are serving those people, because whether these customers show it or not, they are projecting a lot of anticipatory energy—energy we can draw upon to power the level of our performance.

How about Stan the bus driver? This guy has so much power it is incredible. Stan is the not only the person in charge of the vehicle that everyone is contained in, he is the guy who can get people started in the morning on the right foot or not! Stan's effectively in charge of everybody's destiny for that period of time, for one block or one mile. What a responsibility!

Stan reflects into face after face, stop after stop, and has the power to influence as well as to absorb energy from every one of them. Stan can't be creative in the direction his bus takes. His customers wouldn't be too happy if he decided to change his route and take the scenic route through the park one morning. However, Stan can be creative in the way he interacts with his passengers, and that will affect the way he delivers his "performance." Stan doesn't have to look very far to locate his catalyst. If we open our minds and reexamine our job, we may not have to look very far to find ours!

Negativity as a Catalyst

Sometimes it is possible to locate a catalyst in the most unexpected places. I have always found negativity to be a wonderful motivator, a great catalyst. What!? Negativity has redeeming qualities? It's true. When someone has said, "You can't do that," or "You'll never be able to succeed at that," these types of comments have translated into some of the most encouraging challenges I've ever had!

As a teenager, I remember going to one of my first music teachers for a lesson in music theory. Music theory is not something that most guitar players are interested in. Guitarists tend to be more interested in jumping around on stage and drinking and generally going crazy, so it was an uneasy match from the start. The teacher, a wrinkled old grouch who probably turned the majority of her students into toads through some sort of evil spell, ordered me to sit at the piano. She pulled out this sheet of music that looked like the financial section of the *Wall Street Journal*, plunked it down in front of me and commanded, "Play it!"

I had never even sat at a piano yet, much less played one, and I tried to explain to this old wrinkle that I was a guitar player not a pianist. "Never mind!" she said, "Play it!" I looked right into that mass of symbols strewn about the page of music, put both hands down on the keyboard and went for it! Now if you can imagine what a train wreck sounds like, you would get a sense of what old Mrs. Wrinkle heard that day. Keeping in mind what that train wreck sounded like, if you were to imagine what it might have looked like, you would have an idea of that old bag's face when she heard my rendition.

"No, no, no! Not like that—like this."

Then she proceeded to totally humiliate me by banging out some sort of three-handed invention by Ludwig van Beethoven or the like and put my pathetic attempt to shame.

"Now you do it."

"But…"

"Never mind, do it!"

Again I looked at this dog's breakfast on the page of music. I might as well have been reading the Tokyo train time tables for all I knew about written music. "Okay, lady, here it is," I thought, and I proceeded to give her another cascade of musical misery even worse that the first rendition. Then she really let me have it. This wasn't fun any more. I was just a young lad trying to learn something about music theory, I wasn't enlisting in the Marines! This miserable

The cruel music teacher

woman then went into a tirade of vehement and cruel comments about my lack of musical ability.

"You have absolutely no dexterity in your hands whatsoever. You have no musical ability or feeling for music in any way. I strongly discourage you from ever playing a musical instrument of any kind. Good day!"

Needless to say, I was crushed. I couldn't tell anyone what this old woman had said to me. I was totally destroyed by this assessment. And she was supposed to be an authority on the subject! After the tears dried, and I decided *not* to stick my head in the oven, I began to strengthen my resolve. Who made her the big expert anyway?! This event made me even more committed to continue improving my guitar playing in spite of her.

This turned out to be a good thing, because I later ended up working for a number of years as a musician and got to travel all over North America doing it. I met all sorts of interesting people and had the opportunity to play with some very accomplished musicians in many exciting venues. I even made some records and had some of my compositions published by major music publishers. Many times when people applauded for one of my songs or when I received my pay for playing them, I thanked that old bag for indirectly encouraging me to keep after my goal to be a musician.

Although negativity is all around us at times, it can be one of the best sources of motivation available. The catalyst can appear in many different forms and may not look exactly like we expect it to, so watch closely for it, it's out there for us. Let's use it!

NOTEWORTHY SAYS:

- Accept the creative process
- Take risks to stimulate creativity
- We are not peasants, we are performers!
- Utilize the catalyst; it's right in front of us
- Even negativity can serve as a catalyst

⤞ 4 ⤝

POWER TO THE COMMUNICATORS

A person with a strong sense of self-awareness and a good attitude is always employable, but the person with strong communication skills is powerful and promotable. Good communication skills are at the top of the wish list of every employer and headhunter today. Not only are these skills important to our employer, they are critical to our success. Whatever job we have, regardless of our requirements to communicate with customers, we will need to communicate effectively with our supervisors if we intend to advance. We all know how important these skills are—or do we?

Although communication skills are usually the most important aspect of our work, this is generally the area where employees require the most development. Refined communication skills will advance your career faster than anything but marrying the owner of the company (or one of their relatives). For the most part, your actions and your words define who you are. Because it is so important for the people you work with to have a positive "definition" of you, you must use your words wisely.

Learning to Listen

The best way to begin to improve your communication skills is by learning to *listen*. Listen! This may seem very basic, but listening is the key to the most complex interpersonal exchanges. Listening involves more than just noticing that someone is speaking. Listening is an *active* skill requiring you to absorb and sometimes reach to understand not only what is being said, but why. Remember, in order to receive information and to learn something about the individual presenting the information, you must listen.

One of the reasons you may not be listening is that you might take those around you for granted. At the very worst, familiarity breeds contempt and, at best, it breeds complacency. Perhaps you are not expecting to learn anything from certain sources. This is a big mistake, because there is something valuable to be learned from everyone you come in contact with, especially those you work with. As you spend so much time with the people with whom you work, you have a great opportunity to learn from them.

Alternative Sources of Information

Information and ideas can come from the most unexpected places. The accountant in your company may be a source of a lot more than just numbers. That courier, the receptionist, or the door-to-door salesperson may have an important slant to things that you may not have considered. The person at the very bottom of the totem pole can be a critical factor in the scheme of things. Respect this theory! The bottom of the food chain, the plankton in the sea, provides nourishment for much bigger fish. Keep your ears open.

Sometimes we think of things in an orderly, logical fashion rather than from an open, creative perspective. We tend to look to certain sources for certain types of information. For instance, we look for a definition in a dictionary or we try to locate a recipe in a cookbook. We do not think of looking for a definition in a cookbook. Under certain circumstances, the best place to look for a creative new definition just might be in a cookbook!

Hearing is Believing

One barrier to developing our listening skills is that many of us have a tendency to concentrate on our own agendas during discussions. We are not "reading" what the other party is trying to communicate. You may feel that what you have to say is more relevant to the subject, but that may not be the objective of the discussion. When you are listening, you must be assessing not only what the other party is saying, but why. This will put you in a better position to meet your objectives in the conversation.

Talking Through a Mine Field

Avoid the trap of concentrating only on your response during the other person's comment. This is not listening and you may miss important information that will be required for a successful verbal exchange. Sophisticated communication can be like verbal fencing, if you let your guard down to show off, you just might get skewered!

Timing is of the Essence

Another major consideration in communication is *timing*. Content is important, but timing is critical in effective communication. The best idea, the wittiest comment will not be well received if the timing and context are not appropriate. A beautiful French pastry with a great cup of coffee will never be as appetizing before your dinner as it will be when served afterwards.

Social Misdemeanours and Conversation Despots

One way to improve listening skills is to stop talking so much! Silence can be a powerful statement in itself. What better compliment could you receive than "That's the person that only says something when they have something important to say." Sometimes silence can create more impact than a verbal comment.

You don't have to give away the farm in every sentence. Many people commit a social misdemeanour by babbling away incessantly and blocking out any possible slot for reply in the conversation. If you are guilty of this, it will only result in people avoiding you.

If people avoid you, it becomes very difficult to get the valuable information you require to advance. Of course, from time to time all of us may be guilty of talking too much. To guard against this, watch for signals from the other party or parties in the discussion. Are they looking at their watch, are they wiggling in their seats? If they start nodding off while you are talking, perhaps you are not as interesting as you think. Try to be sensitive to their response and do not lull coworkers and managers into a state of rigor mortis.

If you intend to control the conversation, you should have a legitimate objective that will produce a productive result. Here is an example:

A coworker attempts to bog you down with negative comments, issues or complaints, and you do not buy into them. To respond, you take control of the conversation by making a positive comment and then attempt to move the discussion in a more productive direction.

Here is another:

Your manager begins a conversation about an aspect of your work which you are not able to discuss in an informed manner at that moment. Instead of appearing detached or unprepared, you can shift the discussion to an indirectly related issue.

This will "cover" you until you have time to research the issue and reintroduce the conversation later from a greater position of strength. Needless to say, there is a big difference in the subtle use of conversation control than that of the conversation despot's chronic attempts to dominate a discussion.

What's the Objective?

Apart from engaging in small talk, people who have advanced communication skills generally have a specific objective for the outcome of a conversation. The objective may be to give a clear and straightforward message. However, there might be other motives, such as testing for reaction or soliciting a response.

Although they may appear to, an advanced communicator may not be trying to convey a message directly to us at all. They may only be using us as a conduit to pass information on to someone else or to test our confidentiality level. Sometimes what the meaning appears to be on the surface is completely different than the underlying message. By applying listening skills, you can increase your level of perception and begin to hear not only what someone is saying but what they are really communicating. Keep your antenna up and watch body language for additional clues. You want to hone in on what objective is present in your counterpart's communication. You also must be sure to have a clear objective of what you want to communicate before you engage in a discussion.

This is particularly important when you are communicating with managers and supervisors.

One of the best ways to observe advanced communication tactics in action is by listening to politicians. I find this a great way to learn; politicians tend to be excellent communicators, and there is certainly no shortage of material.

Promoting Ourselves

Remember, your job is a vehicle for success and advancement. Ignore what may seem to be restrictions of your position and focus on opportunities to promote yourself. Opportunities for this "promotion" are endless because they occur every time you open your mouth! This does not mean you have a huge neon sign attached to your head flashing "I'm great, check it out—I'm great!" It involves setting the right tone and developing positive momentum which will encompass those around us.

Think of yourself as a nation, a little country of your own. A country that has trade and commerce with many other countries in a huge network of nations. You are an ambassador if you will, to the United States of Me! Therefore, it is important to represent your country in the best possible light at all times. The future of trade and commerce with other nations depends on it!

To Suck Up or Not to Suck Up

There is a distinction between self-promotion and being a "suck." All of us have probably witnessed certain individuals advance to dizzying corporate heights based solely on this method. However, this will not work for most of us and particularly for those of us who are truly interested in self-development.

This is not to say that an encouraging comment or two cast in the direction of your manager at the right moment is totally inappropriate. In fact, as you become more adept in your communications, a subtle "stroke" can be a good prelude to opening your agenda within a conversation. Baking cakes and cookies for the boss goes a little too far in my opinion, but it has worked for some. I believe that it is more important to maintain one's self-respect and develop more sophisticated communication techniques than to simply suck up to managers.

Relationships at Work

Here are some guidelines for relationships at work:

- The most common error people make is wanting to be liked by everyone. This is an unrealistic goal and basically impossible to attain. A more practical goal is to be liked by some and respected by most.

- We must separate personal relationships and working relationships, as they have entirely different functions and exist for different reasons.

- Exercise caution when developing personal relationships with supervisors. Although these relationships may have short-term benefits, they have a tendency to backfire in the long term.

- Avoid romantic relationships at work unless you are prepared to seek employment elsewhere. Otherwise you take the risk of making yourself and the rest of your coworkers miserable in the interim.

Communicating with Managers, Supervisors and Institutions

When we communicate with those who are higher than us in the "food chain," we want to neutralize the difference in our positions as much as possible. Avoid buying into the "Wizard of Oz Syndrome" of assuming you and other staff members are on different levels. This is not to say that you should not show respect for your manager or their position. The objective here is to detach the institution from the person.

We want to disconnect the person from their position and allow the communication to proceed to a more intimate level: person-to-person as opposed to employer/employee or lord-to-peasant. When communication is moved to a more personal level, you will have more control over the situation and be in a position to enhance your message by injecting your personality. You will be able to attach more weight to your message and have a much greater chance of "hitting home." Utilizing this system will yield much better results than dealing from a position of weakness fostered by the traditional employer/employee relationship. To simplify, the objective is to "humanize" our communications with those in power.

Humour as a Communicator

When I began my career in the field of business training, I remember that first day at work. I eagerly set out to look my best and to perform my best, just like any of us would on that all-important first day on the job. As I was on my way into the office to start my new career, I stopped at the men's room to get myself on track. After all, I had three cups of coffee that morning to get myself pumped up for that burst off the starting line. As I stepped up to my place at the urinal, I gave little thought to the very tall man pumped up for that burst off the starting line. As I stepped up to my place at the urinal, I gave little thought to the very tall man standing next to me and I carried on with my business without acknowledging him. As I reached for the handle of the urinal to flush it, the washer in the handle mechanism must have broken because water started spraying in every direction all over both of us!

Although I consider myself to be a disciplined person, I *am* human and I directed an eloquent blue streak of comments toward that urinal. I was compelled to do this, partly to relieve my anger at this ridiculous situation and partly to deflect the blame for the benefit of the large gentleman I had inadvertently sprayed. He seemed to take it a lot better than I did, he blotted his sleeve with a paper towel and silently left the washroom. Well of course he could take it better than I could, he only had a light misting and I looked like I required a catheter! I was a complete mess, my pants were soaked and I was starting a new job in a few minutes! Some first impression I was about to make!

Thank goodness there was a multidirectional hot air powered hand dryer in the facility. It was time to be creative, so I attempted to at least dry off my slacks. After a few minutes I got a reasonable job done and although I was now late, I didn't appear to have any major medical problems requiring immediate attention.

I have no idea what the other patrons of that washroom thought I was up to but I was certainly providing more than my share of entertainment for the day. It was too late for embarrassment now, I had a career to begin. I tried to collect myself, left the washroom and made my entrance through the door to my new job. As I entered the office, the first person I made eye contact with was, you guessed it, the large man who I had earlier sprayed in the washroom. "Good morning, I am the principal of the school, how can I help you?" he said as he held out his hand to greet me.

Great, the guy I had just watered down in the bathroom was going to be my new boss! Not only that, this big fella' had just been exposed to one of the more articulate organizations of angry expletives I had ever delivered. I held out my hand to accept his greeting and said, "It's all right, it's dry," and as our hands met, there was a long frozen pause. As the pause ended, the ice shattered and we simultaneously burst into laughter.

Humour can bridge differences in opinion, mend fences and rescue us from the most awkward situations. Humour is one of the best tools of advanced communicators. Everybody loves a good laugh, some comic relief, or a humorous approach to things. There is even a complex physiological process we undergo when we laugh that makes us feel better.

Humour in the workplace can be the most enjoyable part of coming to work each day. Saying something humorous to put someone at ease or to add some levity to an otherwise dismal situation can be very productive. Furthermore, a keen wit is a very appealing quality in a person; people love to be around someone who makes them feel good.

A well-placed witty remark can be something that people will remember you for long after they have forgotten the discussion itself. The right punch line to punctuate a message you are trying to convey or something that hit the funny bone in the midst of a more serious presentation can have an incredibly powerful impact.

Atoms & Elements

People are the heart and soul of every organization. They are the biggest part of what makes a job worth loving. Apart from learning volumes from our coworkers, we are in a position to develop lifelong connections with people whom we might not otherwise come into contact with. And it's the contact with all these different personalities that can make our work so interesting.

Each of us is the nucleus of our own sphere of influence—like microscopic atomic solar systems with you at the centre of their orbit. When the orbits of certain atoms interface with the orbits of other atoms they create different elements. For instance, hydrogen and oxygen create water (H_2O).

In the same way, when a person's orbit of influence interfaces with the orbit of another person, a new "element" is created. Some groups of atoms combine to create gold or silver, while others interact to create inert gasses and dense base metals! The same principle can be applied to personal interaction. Make sure you are bonding with those that produce precious metals and avoid the gasses! Seek out the winners and try to connect with them. Observe and learn from them, they have power that can be absorbed and tapped into if you take advantage of it. That connection could be as good as gold.

Politics at Work (Keep Your Friends Close and Your Enemies Closer)

Many people will tell you to avoid politics at work. Sometimes this may be good advice, but if you are to advance yourself, you must at least respect politics in the workplace. No matter what you think about the dramas that swirl around you, they will never go away. They are as much of an inextricable part of working as people are. It is important to differentiate between politics that help and politics that hurt us. Begin by determining who will be helpful to your advancement and who will be detrimental to your success.

Make sure that you are reciprocating favours and supporting

those who are helpful. With those who are potentially detrimental, try to swallow your pride and attempt to improve your rapport with them whenever the opportunity arises. Otherwise, stay proud and avoid these people. Returning to the "United States of Me" theory, you want to have good relations with the other nations. Where good relations are difficult, at least have working treaties.

Behavioural Imprints

Whether we realize it or not, each one of us is a nucleus of energy, ideas, and talent. We have varying degrees of impact on everything and everyone we come in contact with. That impact could be generally put into three categories:

Positive   +

Neutral   o

Negative   –

An example of something that creates a positive impact would be adding something to the working environment or the work itself. For instance, complimenting a coworker on a job well done. Or coming up with a way for the company to save time or money on any level of its operation. An example of something that creates a neutral impact would be just continuing to do what you need to do to get things done—no more, no less, no changes, no waves; just keep plugging away. Actions that create negative impact are things like a lack of enthusiasm on the job or poor interaction with coworkers.

Just as we leave fingerprints on everything we touch, our behaviour leaves an *imprint* on everyone around us. Conversely, the behaviour of others around us can leave its imprint on us. Each word, each action we make not only defines us, it has an effect on those around us. This is an important concept, because if you consistently have a positive impact on others, you will eventually be the recipient of those positive actions returning to you.

Behaviour can be contagious and has a tendency to travel in a circle. This circle produces momentum. Developing positive momentum is a gradual process that takes time before you see a return on your investment. The return will come, and when it does, you will have demonstrated leadership that will be recognized and appreciated by those around you. This return will be worth waiting for, because once this momentum is established it will carry you even farther down the road to greater success in your job.

WAYS TO CREATE POSITIVE IMPACT:

- ❑ Being helpful to coworkers
- ❑ Be optimistic
- ❑ Ask for advice on tasks
- ❑ Use advice given
- ❑ Accept constructive criticism and act on it
- ❑ Encourage others
- ❑ *Always* give cheerful salutations

Setting the Tone

Remember that the level of professionalism—the standard you set in your behaviour—will be reflected by those with whom you interact. This means that you can influence the level of professionalism of others around you. In fact, you have a lot more impact in this area than you might think. How does it work? It starts with making a commitment to behaving in a professional, ethical manner at all times. That means being consistently professional in the way you present yourself. It is a long-term process that begins by exercising the discipline required to develop consistency. This is known as building *credibility*.

Most forms of employment provide the opportunity to develop credibility. Take advantage of that opportunity, because credibility is a completely bankable benefit of the job. The big bonus is that credibility is portable within an industry; it is something that you can take with you to the next job. Because of this portability factor, it is well worth devoting time to developing credibility.

NOTEWORTHY SAYS:

- Listening is one of the most important communication tools

- When you speak, have an objective

- Promote yourself without "sucking up"

- Humour is a powerful communicator

- Respect politics at work

- Generate positive momentum; it travels in a circle

- Invest time in developing credibility

∽ 5 ∾

IMAGE BUILDING

It was midnight blue, I'm sure, sleek and low to the ground. The cool cruiser shone in the sunlight as it pulled up to the curb beside me. The window slid down, and in the passenger seat sat the most beautiful girl I had ever seen. In the driver's seat was my guitar teacher, Eddie. He was a tall guy, about thirty, wearing a long black leather jacket; he had very bad skin. Eddie may have been a criminal—a pimp for all I knew—but being a middle class kid, about thirteen, I didn't know what those things were, so it didn't concern me.

All I knew was that Eddie had a lot of charisma. I don't remember him being able to play the guitar very well; in fact I don't remember much about those music lessons. However, I do remember that Eddie had a lot of raw confidence and I was very impressed by his "style." Because Eddie was a musician, whatever he said was important. At least it was to me, because when I was growing up, all I ever wanted was to be a musician. These guys had all the fun, got all the girls and seemed to do whatever they wanted. And they got paid to do it! Musicians even looked better than everybody else (except for Eddie). Not only had I met someone who appeared to be a real live musician, he was actually my music teacher. Compared to the square teachers at my school, Eddie seemed to be plugged into something, had something going that the others didn't have. What was it?

Looking back at this phenomenon, I now understand that I was getting my first exposure to image development and charismatic projection. Eddie had a role that he played very well and it allowed him to achieve his desired goals. Taken out of context, Eddie may have seemed quite silly, but at that moment he was able to project confidence and get his message across to people.

Perception is Everything

It has been proven time and time again that through a bit of marketing magic and a developed image, individuals with limited talent but an abundance of confidence have been able to become incredibly successful. *Do not underestimate this principle.* One of the few people to serve two consecutive terms as President of the United States was a mediocre actor!

At birth we are dealt a hand governed strictly by genetics and destiny, and that's what we end up with, right? No! We are in a position to change more things around us than you might think. Long before people have an opportunity to get to know who we are and what we are really capable of, they formulate their opinions of us based on the perception or image of who we are.

The perception people have of you is critical. With a bit of imagination, it is easier to create the perception than the substance. You will, of course, require some substance sooner or later, but in order to get your foot in opportunity's door, creating the correct perception will go far in getting you started. It will also buy you the time you need to develop the required substance.

Above all, you want to create the perception that you are successful. A good personal appearance is one of the best ways to create the professional and successful image you want to portray. I have always believed that the best investment a person can make is in clothing. The better you look, the better you feel. When you feel good about yourself, others pick up on it and you will have a positive impact on those around you. No matter what you look like on paper, always look good in person.

Only the most successful person can afford to dress like a bum. While building your success, you must do everything you can to appear as successful as possible. Another example of the importance of perception is: you will never be paid what you are worth, you will only be paid what people think you are worth!

Confidence Building

The most important part of a successful image is confidence. When we are at work we must try to project as much confidence as possible. At certain times it is more difficult to achieve this, and some situations require displaying more confidence than others.

Here is one confidence-building technique:

Before you negotiate a raise in salary, have a critical meeting or a make a major presentation of any kind, try this visualization technique. Imagine that you're sitting on two or three hundred thousand bucks in term deposits, treasury bills or cash in your bank account. Just visualize how you might feel if you had that kind of power and financial security. If you had that much money, you wouldn't need the approval of your boss or your clients on your next move, would you? Exactly!

If you can create the perception that you're not hungry, that you don't need what your counterpart in the situation has to offer, you will be perceived as being more confident because you are dealing from a position of strength. Confidence can be self-generating if you can put certain thoughts and feelings in motion. Remember the term deposits and treasury bills. Have you ever noticed that people who have money and power have confidence? Of course they do, they can afford to be confident!

You need to have the ability to appear as confident as those powerful people. If you can generate the confidence, although you may not be powerful, you can create the appearance of success and you will have a better chance to achieve the desired outcome in your negotiations or presentations. This is not magic! This is a matter of developing your technique. Refinement of the technique will come with practise, just like learning how to play the piano.

Draw on your personal experiences to give you the strength required to project confidence. If you do not have many of your own experiences yet to draw on, read biographies of successful people. Try to imagine the obstacles they overcame to achieve their success and compare those obstacles to the ones facing you. There are many successful people in business, sports, and entertainment to draw upon for inspiration to generate confidence. This is not to say that you will become Lee Iacocca just by reading about him and thinking about him before you have an important meeting. However, by understanding more about how Iacocca overcame obstacles and persevered to become successful, you can apply some of the same principles of determination and positive thinking to help you create the required perception.

Acting confidently and being confident can produce the same results. How many times have you seen an actor or performer interviewed while "out of character" and observed how shy or introverted they are? They certainly have confidence in their craft, but they don't continuously display it. When you see them acting out their part or observe their stage "persona," they seem or become an entirely different character.

Just as an accomplished actor totally immerses himself in a character, you can take on the role of a confident individual. Play the part to your audience—your boss, your coworkers and your customers. The ability to play that part will improve with practise, just as a great actor's does. Once you get used to the feeling of playing the part, you will actually become more confident. And you can have a lot of fun doing it!

This theory is best applied to new contacts and customers. When you meet someone for the first time they have no idea who you are or what your position in the world is. The only way they can make an assessment about you is by using the information you give them. Information communicated in the way you carry yourself, the way you express your ideas and your reaction to various situations. If you can successfully portray that confident character and be observed doing so, it will produce positive results.

Try to get into your confident character in the same way a great actor immerses herself into a role to successfully "sell" her audience the belief that she *is* the character. Remember, confidence is important, but creating the perception of being confident is even more important. If you can create the illusion of confidence, you will become more confident in the process.

Dealing With Rejection

A major part of becoming more confident is learning how to deal with rejection. I learned a major lesson on the subject many years ago.

Having spent a number of years as a musician, one of the benefits I was able to enjoy was the opportunity to travel. I was fortunate enough to see many places that I might not otherwise had the chance or the desire to see. During one tour, one of the stops was Whitehorse, in the Yukon. Returning to the Canadian North generated a certain nostalgia, almost a smugness, as this time I came as a musician rather than a rookie mill worker. However, as glad as I was to revisit the frozen north, it turned out that the feeling was not exactly mutual.

One of the more complicated aspects of the business of a touring band is the phenomenon known as the "booking agent." The first priority of the booking agent is the commission he receives every time he provides entertainment for various venues. Among the lower priorities are things like the compatibility of the venue to the act and, conversely, the act to the venue. Unfortunately, on this tour it would be my band that was the victim of this discrepancy in priorities.

Canadian "Outback" inhabitants in 1972 were hungry—in fact, starved—for culture and entertainment. (Our act fit in somewhere between the two). Although the patrons of the local establishments are fiercely enthusiastic about any form of live music, they are equally unforgiving if it does not fall into a narrow range of what they consider to be entertaining. In that era, it fell somewhere between Elvis and strippers.

We were going to have extreme difficulties fitting into this range, as our music was a very progressive blend of rhythm-and-blues and jazz. Put our two African-American singers into the mix and this was an entree that would prove a little hard for the locals to digest. This is not to say the locals lacked any degree of polish; it was just their missing teeth and those large power tools they brought into the club that tended to be a tad distracting.

Coming from a bigger city like Vancouver and looking out onto such an audience the first night of our engagement generated a certain apprehension. However, as we were committed to perform for three weeks in this venue, it was no time to be squeamish. The show must go on! In spite of some resistance to our opening numbers, we proceeded to take the program further into uncharted avant garde territories! The patrons took to their feet and began hurling comments. As the atmosphere became increasing volatile, projectiles followed.

At that point, I don't know what came over me, but I remember shouting into the microphone something like "You didn't pay to get in here so you won't have to pay to get out ... so why not get the hell out!" Just as I said that, the room reached a kindling point and the joint erupted. Within seconds the customers started rushing up to front of the stage shouting things like, "Let's give it to 'em" and "Fix those city slickers!"

It was now time to fall back onto some of the training I acquired at the mine. I grabbed my guitar and started running! We ran to the back of the stage where the dressing room was located and barricaded ourselves in. Meanwhile, one of the braver band members stayed behind and was swinging a microphone stand at the oncoming patrons. Fortunately some members of the Royal Canadian Mounted Police were just arriving on one of their routine visits to the local watering holes and saved us in the nick of time.

Rejection hurts no matter what the situation. No one likes it. However, rejection doesn't hurt as much as a power tool applied to one's arms or legs! Remember this story the next time you are about to give an important presentation or have a great idea you want to share with your manager. If you are not that well received for one reason or another, at least you will not be literally running for your life as a result of it.

We have to keep things in perspective when dealing with rejection. Although at the time you may feel that this is the worst thing that could ever happen to anyone, it is not. Even my horror story of rejection will pale to another. Stay focused on your goal and keep on going no matter what!

NOTEWORTHY SAYS:

* Perception can mean everything

* You will never be paid what you are worth, only what people think you are worth

* Character acting can build confidence

* Try to be objective when dealing with rejection

∞ 6 ∞

WORKING AT NETWORKING

We're working at improving our communication skills, we're developing a confident image, and now we can move forward. We have established that, even if our current job leaves a lot to be desired, it can be an important part of our career path. We discussed interaction with coworkers earlier, so let's go on to the next step. Let's explore expanding our interactions beyond the realm of our employment.

Imagine looking up into the sky on a clear night and observing all the stars shining above you. Think of all of the solar systems and galaxies that connect with one another for as far as your imagination will take you. Back on Earth, each one of us is the centre of our own galaxy, the centre of an important *personal sphere of influence* or network.

The Network

Just as the orbits (networks) of interplanetary systems intersect with orbits of many other systems, our personal sphere of influence intersects with an unending number of other spheres of influence. Many of these spheres have the potential to have an enormous impact on our career. However, the potential can never be realized unless we are prepared to take risks and venture out of our familiar, comfortable orbit to follow and explore these intersecting orbits.

Before we begin the journey out of our orbit, we will need some special equipment to sustain us on our trek into the unknown. The first tool we will require is *optimism*. We must remain optimistic that our journey will produce positive results. Optimistic, in that we will not feel that we have wasted our time if our journey does not yield immediate returns. We will also need to make the commitment to exercise optimism no matter what happens on our adventure. We must reassure ourselves that regardless of the outcome, we will have benefited and grown by showing the courage to venture into the unknown.

The next tool we will need is *patience*. Before we will be able to realize the benefits of our journey, we will require patience. Cultivating new contacts takes time and effort. We must be patient for the seeds we have planted on new worlds to grow and bear fruit. We must also understand that the other spheres we will come into contact with will have their own timetables, which will operate completely independently of our timetable.

Another tool we will need for the trip outside our galaxy is *discipline*, discipline to use the information we gather on our journey in a positive, constructive and ethical way. We will also need the discipline necessary to steer us away from the comfort of what we know and thrust ourselves into the unknown. Discipline to keep forging ahead through occasional deserts void of worthwhile contacts. Discipline to maintain the stamina we will require to discover our oases of mentors, benefactors and opportunities that lie ahead.

One thing we don't have to bring too much of with us will be *expectations.* If we have too many expectations, it can stunt the natural development of our network. These unknown orbits can take us in many directions. If we presuppose the outcome before we begin, it will influence the distance and direction of our journey.

What will happen and where we will end up is completely unknown. If we already know what the adventure is all about, we don't need to go on it. Instead of expectations, let's take some long-term *goals* with us on the trip. Having goals for what we hope to accomplish is a much better choice of luggage for the expedition. Our goals will serve as the best navigator, as expectations have a tendency to steer us toward preconceived destinations.

Now that we have packed our 'interplanetary tool kit' with a few essential items, we can begin the journey out of our orbit. We can now undertake our adventure in a self-assured fashion because when we are prepared we will become confident. Before we strike out on our journey, let's read this true story of what can happen to someone when they step out of their familiar orbit to boldly explore new worlds.

Ups And Downs

In one of my many careers, I worked as a piano salesman. At the time I was in the piano business, it was an interesting and relatively lucrative field. A piano, especially a grand piano, is a big ticket item, and a piano salesperson can do well if his or her business is built on a core of solid clients.

One of the benefits of selling pianos was the opportunity to come in contact with influential people, people who feel they must have a glistening, black grand piano in their home as a symbol of prestige—a line of thinking that I support totally. However, one of the drawbacks was having to lift the pianos off a truck, uncrate and carry them out into the showroom for display. I had already witnessed injurious manual labour at the mine, and after a grand piano fell off the truck and narrowly missed my head, I was inspired to quickly activate my network to seek new professional endeavours.

One of my customers was a successful manager of the local branch of a national brokerage firm. I had developed a good rapport with him and he had commented favourably on my sales ability at least once. Although I had little background in the financial industry, I figured that selling one thing was the same as another, so I started pestering my customer to give me a job as a stockbroker.

Although I was initially unsuccessful, I remained optimistic that my networking would eventually pay off, and I was patient as I continued to learn everything I could about the securities industry. I was beginning to develop a preoccupation with the stock market. As a musician, I had always been fascinated by numbers and mathematics. The idea of making money from buying and selling paper with the mine's name on it was a lot more appealing than wielding a pneumatic drill at the bottom of *the mine itself!* I studied a securities course at night after work and began reading every book about the stock market I could get my hands on.

My interest was now at a peak and I was dying to play the market. I began bothering another one of my customers (also a stockbroker) to consider taking me on as one of his clients. He finally agreed, reluctantly, to let me invest my life savings of a thousand dollars in the stock market. He proceeded to recommend a speculative oil and gas stock which I purchased at forty cents a share.

I continued working at the piano store and kept studying for the securities course. As I was working away, that little stock started to increase in value. I religiously followed its progress in the business section of the paper every day. Up five cents, then up ten cents, and so on. I would phone my stockbroker and ask him, "Is it going higher?" And he would reply "It's going higher." This was all pretty exciting for a young lad who had put his life savings into some unknown little oil stock. Before long I had saved up another thousand dollars and again my broker reluctantly agreed to let me invest it in more of the same stock. By this time the stock was about $1.50, but nevertheless, I happily paid the price to get more of the best thing since sliced bread.

Things continued on in the same way; I would look in the paper in the morning and see up ten cents, up fifteen, and have a warm feeling as I sipped my coffee. I scrimped and saved and sold as many pianos as I could so I would make as much money as possible. Money which would enable me to buy more stock. I was getting wired to it, but it wasn't a bad thing because the stock just kept going up— up twenty, up twenty-five, and on and on. Meanwhile, although I kept on studying, I failed my first attempt at the securities exam so I was still not much closer to my goal of becoming a stockbroker. However, that little stock was now over ten dollars and was going plus fifty, plus seventy-five, plus a dollar! This was better than sliced bread—this was the whole loaf!

About this time I discovered what is known as the "margin" account. Buying on margin basically amounts to borrowing money against the stock you have in your account to buy more stock. If that stock goes up you get to margin even more and buy more stock by borrowing against the gain on the previous purchase. This was great—pretty soon the stock was up over twenty dollars and, because of that amazing margin account, I had quite a bit of it. At this point I didn't understand how or why this was all happening; all I knew was this stock was only going in one direction, right to the moon, and I needed to get my hands on more of it!

To get a feel for the financial climate in those days, you have to appreciate that, in the late seventies, the banks were pretty loose with their money. Prosperity seemed like it was around every corner. Real estate was up, stocks were up. There didn't seem to be any end in sight. The bankers were more interested in the commissions they received from writing loans than they were in security or collateral. One of my contacts knew one such banker who was interested in developing new accounts with up-and-coming professionals.

Thanks to an introduction, I met with that banker and before I knew it, I had a $20,000 line of credit! This was great because I could take this $20,000 and put it into a margin account and then borrow against that money and buy even more stock!!

The only problem with this unfolding drama was that my broker thought I was getting too deep into this stock. "Isn't it going higher?" I asked. "It's going higher," he would say. I couldn't understand. If the stock was going higher, why didn't he want me to get in on it? There was only one thing to do about this little snag. I contacted my other customer, the stockbroker I had been bugging for a job and got him to open an account for me with his firm.

"$20,000, that's quite a bit of money for a young fella'. You must be doing pretty good at that piano store." He said.

"You betcha'" I replied.

"So, what do you wanna' do with this account?"

"I want to put it all into this stock, at full margin!"

"Are you nuts?"

"Nope."

"Okay. It's your money."

This turned out to be perfect because I now had two brokers watching the stock for me. And when the stock went to thirty dollars shortly after I opened the account with the second broker, my prospective employer, I suddenly looked like a real genius!

In fact, I was on such a roll, I ordered some nice made-to-measure suits. Not only that, I went out and bought a brand-spanking new, top-of-the-line, jet-black Oldsmobile! Now that was a real car! In those days an Oldsmobile was like a big fancy couch with shiny chrome wire wheels on it. Now that I had my new suits and my big black car, I was starting to look a lot better to my customer, the manager of the brokerage firm. Not to mention that he was putting his clients into that stock and as it had now moved up to around $38, he was looking pretty good too. Everything was working out so well that he finally offered me the job I had wanted so badly.

I was now faced with a dilemma. I hadn't passed the securities course yet because I was busy with other things like eating out at gourmet restaurants and drinking champagne in the Jockey Club at the race track. However, I was sure I would eventually pass that darned exam, and if I took the job, at the very least I would be able to look after my own account. After about 45 seconds of deliberation, I accepted the offer, but with one condition. I was going on a short seven-week holiday through California, Las Vegas, the Bahamas and down to the island of Martinique, near Venezuela.

"What?!" exclaimed my new employer.

"I'm going to be pretty busy selling that hot stock to all my new clients when I start so I better rest while I can." I replied.

"All right, but you better pass that securities exam when you get back."

"No problem." I replied, and off I went.

With my jeans thoroughly stuffed with cash, I embarked on

the journey of a lifetime. After the allotted time, I arrived back east at the "training centre" fat, bronzed and sassy! Needless to say, it was somewhat difficult to fit into the "training" program, sitting with a handful of rookies listening to how to become successful in the stock market.

I generally left the "training" sessions early and returned to the hotel for champagne and banana flambé or to chat with the little Italian tailor I consigned to make some new suits for me. My lifestyle was in mild conflict with that of the anal pinstripes from the East, but that only encouraged me to continue my lavish lifestyle and to keep charging it to the company-sponsored hotel.

It didn't take long for word to get back home that there was some rookie acting like Howard Hughes, carrying on at the training centre like there was no tomorrow. I was immediately brought back home to report to the office manager and start my new job. Although my new employers had some problems with my high profile approach, I was sure I had learned a lot more than I was given credit for. My style of learning was just a little different than that of the pinstripes, that's all.

Back home, life was great. I drove my shiny black Oldsmobile to the big office tower downtown and pulled into my own parking spot every day. I began putting my friends, my relatives, and all my contacts, especially the influential ones with the grand pianos, into that little gold mine of a stock that had treated me so well. In the evenings after work, I would go to swanky restaurants and enjoy great food and wine. As I carved my rack of lamb or smoked my big Cuban cigar, I would reflect on how far I had come from the "cook shack" at the mine only a few years earlier.

Things continued in this rosy fashion for some time, until one day something very different occurred. I was sitting at my desk thinking about my next vacation while watching the monitor that displayed the stocks. At that time, the stocks were not shown on the screen the way they are today. The monitor showed the actual floor of the exchange where you would watch the "markers" write the prices (bid and ask) of the stock on the board in felt pen. As the prices changed, the markers would erase the old quote and put up the new one.

My stock was pretty steady in the forty-dollar range, and I watched it trade with confidence, day in and day out. That day, as I looked over at the monitor, I happened to notice a flurry of activity around one of the markers. Suddenly I realized that the drama being generated was swirling around MY STOCK! I saw the marker write $34, and quickly replace it with $32, then $27! Wait a minute! People were running around the office screaming that the market on my stock was crashing! Of course everyone in the place was interested in that stock because I had the other brokers and all of the office staff invested in it! The announcement of halt trading came crackling over the speaker system in the office. The order was issued by the stock exchange to clarify trading "irregularities" and a pending announcement.

When trading of a stock is halted, there is no activity. No buying, no selling, nothing. When trading is halted because of negative information coming out on a company, a lot of attention is attracted to the stock. Consequently, the owners and brokers of that stock are usually lined up at the exits waiting to get out of the stock. This results in increased downward pressure on the price of the stock and when it eventually resumes trading, it can result in a complete collapse of the price. A halt trading order can be one of the most frightening events to occur in the life of a stock trader if they are on the wrong side of a trade.

Trading was suspended until the trading session the following day. I spent the longest night of my life awaiting the news. I was totally unglued by these events—this stock was only supposed to go one way! I was in denial; this couldn't be happening. As I watched the monitor the next day when trading resumed, I was dumbfounded, paralyzed as the price tumbled. I couldn't sell, I wouldn't! The stock was supposed to go back up just as it always had before.

This time it wasn't coming back. The word on the street was the company was simply a shell with no assets or business activities to speak of, it was just a vehicle for speculation. After the outrage and scandal that took place over the following days and weeks, the stock finally settled at about forty cents. Needless to say, I was devastated. This unfortunate series of events was even further compounded as, shortly afterward, financial markets around the world fell into a great decline and we entered one of the worst recessions in history.

This was the end of my career as a stock broker. I got caught in the oldest game in the book. It's called "watch the rookie blow his brains out." It happens when some fresh young recruit puts all his money in a high-flying stock and then proceeds to load all his friends and relatives into the same high risk deal—and then the bottom of the market falls out. Ouch!

The Moral of the Story

A lot has happened in my career path since then, but what clearly remains is the vivid illustration of the potentially amazing outcomes that can be reached by exploring networks—spheres of influence that are constantly accessible and available to each of us.

Unfortunately, in my case, I used only two of the three tools we require for a successful journey out of orbit to contact outlying spheres of influence. Although the outcome was a series of some of my most interesting experiences to date, I failed to exercise *discipline*. The knowledge and power that I had gained was not used in a constructive way. I was certainly *optimistic* about the potential outcome. I was *patient* and kept after my desire to be an investor and a stockbroker. However, beyond that, I had no long-term goal other than to obtain unlimited wealth in a short period of time, which was an unrealistic *expectation*. If I had been better prepared and had taken the right tools on the journey, this story would have had an altogether different outcome.

The most important point of this story is that if I hadn't undertaken the adventure in the first place, I would have missed a cornucopia of opportunities. Although the story didn't have a textbook ending, I learned a great deal about financial markets, as well as fine dining, vintage wines, Cuban cigars and horse racing!

Not only can networking lead to improving your job, it can take you farther than you expected. For all of us there is a universe of experiences out there waiting to be discovered. It is as close as that first step out of your familiar orbit into the many surrounding spheres of influence. The networks are all around us, let's start intersecting!!

NOTEWORTHY SAYS:

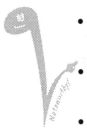

- There are many networks/spheres of influence around all of us that can offer great opportunities

- Before you go out of your orbit remember to "pack" optimism, patience, and discipline

- Use your goals, not your expectations, as your navigator

Don't be afraid of the unknown.
Welcome it.
Taking risks can pay off bigtime.

∽ **7** ∾

NICE GUYS FINISH …

Why does it seem like many of the most ruthless people are the most successful? Because they are!! How do you think they got to be so successful? They don't get into a deal to help the other guy out, they are in there to win! If they were waiting around for someone to make them successful, they wouldn't be where they are today, at the top of the food chain.

When I think of the Captains of Industry or the deal-makers of the century, I have a vision of the Viking warriors marching into a village, slashing, burning and pillaging, taking no prisoners. At the end of the campaign, the only things that remain are the spoils of conflict and the Viking banner standing proudly above all.

Do we need to be as cruel and vicious as the Vikings to advance in our careers? Let's hope not. However, there are pages from the Viking's book of triumph that we can utilize to move up in the food chain. The biggest advantage that the Vikings of contemporary industry have over us is that they don't have consciences getting in the way of their progress. They know that they come first, that winning is everything and nothing else really matters.

Fortunately, this line of thinking will be alien to many of us. We are more sensitive, more genteel than the Vikings. While most of us desire the acknowledgment and the trappings that success has to offer, we can't quite see ourselves mercilessly tearing the flesh off the backs of our coworkers and contacts to get it. We take pride in our ethics and enjoy the benefits of a good night's sleep.

Although the Vikings' methods leave something to be desired, they did some things right. Let's see if we can take some of the shine from the sword of those victorious warriors without having to do quite as much hacking and hewing. The important thing to be gleaned from the Vikings is their attitude rather than their actions. The mind set that you are going to succeed—to prevail no matter what obstacle presents itself—is a good framework in which to operate. This focus will allow us to direct our energies toward our goal without having to lop off the arms and legs of everyone around us. We want to incorporate an "I win, you win" scenario as opposed to the Viking's "I win, you lose" approach.

In order to move ahead, it is not necessary to go out of the way to step on others; leave that to the Vikings. However, in our career path we will arrive at crossroads at which we must make critical decisions as to whose interests come first. We will have to make decisions that relate to our success and to our very survival. Let's clearly separate the two issues. Remember, before we can succeed, we must first survive. When it comes down to survival, we must fearlessly conquer the opposition, just like the Vikings. In matters of building our success, we must be careful to balance compassion and ambition and to keep each of them in their proper perspective.

If we live by the motto "I win, you win," we will do well; but if we live by this code alone, we will not reach the lofty heights that we aspire to. It's true—if we want to succeed, we need those around us as much as they need us. But let's accept the fact that we need some people more than others. (Remember the Atoms and Elements from Chapter Four, "Power to the Communicators.") As we are cultivating the corporate ground in which we hope to grow more powerful, we also need to cultivate the ground of our coworkers.

Although the vast majority of coworkers will respond favourably to this nurturing process, there will be a very small minority who will not and who may need to be weeded out of the corporate ground that we have tended so lovingly.

As I mentioned earlier, there will be occasions in which we will be forced to make decisions that will have long-term impact on our careers. When these decisions involve the prospect of choosing our advancement at the expense of others, we must carefully weigh the potential outcomes. As much as we want others around us to succeed, there will be times (hopefully, very few of them) when we must lift our sword and spill a little blood on that corporate ground. Don't be shocked, at times this is WAR! We will never go out of our way to hurt others (professionally speaking of course), but there has never been a battle won without casualties. When necessary, let's act first and make sure that we are never counted among them!! Of course our motto is still "I win, you win." But when it comes to the "weeds," it's going to have to become "I win, you lose." Don't feel bad about it, they were going to lose anyway, we just helped them out the door and on their way so they could lose somewhere else.

Lovers or Warriors ?

Consider the story of Connie. Connie meant well enough, but she had an abysmal attitude. Every day she came to work, Connie brought a face that looked like it just bit into a lemon. That is, on the days that she came in to work at all. Connie's absenteeism was very high because not only was her professional life in trouble, her personal life was a mess as well.

As most of us who worked in the same office were positive, good-natured people, this was not a great match of personalities. Try as we might to get her pumped up, we were not successful. Connie's misery was a bottomless black hole that could engulf the goodwill and warm feelings of Santa himself. We tried to like Connie. It shouldn't have been that difficult, we liked everybody! Although all of us wished she would go away, we didn't have the heart to have her fired. After all, she was efficient enough when she did show up for work. Besides, we were basically lovers, not warriors. We gave people the benefit of the doubt until the very end and then some.

One thing that Connie was very good at was complaining about how she was not being paid enough. As we heard this complaint over and over like a mantra, we began to get an idea. We decided to start researching the job market to find a position that would be more financially rewarding for Connie. Instead of propping her up by resisting her negative comments, we began to agree with her arguments and encouraged her to look for a job more suited to her abilities. We even did some job prospecting for Connie and passed the leads directly on to her.

In spite of her weaknesses, she was efficient and could probably fool anyone initially. She had fooled us, after all, we hired her. It would only be later when the smoke started to clear at her new job and she started turning on her new coworkers, that she would be discovered. By then it would be too late! It would be someone else's problem.

We kept at it diligently, and it eventually worked like a charm. Connie began to go out to various job interviews with all of us cheering her on every step of the way. Eventually it happened. Connie was offered another job which she finally accepted, although at one point she became reluctant to leave such a friendly, supportive group of coworkers! Fortunately the hesitation was short-lived, and she rode quietly away into the sunset never to be seen again.

Wicked? Devious? Manipulative? Of course! This was a matter of survival. It was either going to be Connie or the rest of us. Thankfully, it was Connie who left and the remaining members of the staff lived happily to tell of it. Hardly slash-and-burn tactics of the Vikings, but an effective way to weed out a nonproductive, negative force in an otherwise positive working environment. Most of us are lovers, not warriors; but when it comes down to survival, the tough get tougher and the losers get the highway.

Declaration of Success

As we set out on our course to advance ourselves in our job, our actions will not only be noticed by our employers, but by our coworkers as well. The impact of our actions can present some problems we should become aware of right from the start.

When we have resolved within ourselves that we are going to love our job and to get it working for us, we will have effectively made a "Declaration of Success." That is, we will be declaring ourselves as to the direction we intend our career to take. Needless to say, that direction is aimed straight for the top. Although this is essentially an internal commitment to ourselves, the actions resulting from that commitment will have an external effect on those around us. For example, if we were to quit smoking or go on a diet, our internal commitment to changing our behaviour will generate external reaction to these changes by others.

When we make a commitment or a declaration regarding our career future, there is likely to be some potentially negative repercussions from some of our coworkers. Why? Because one of the unfortunate sides of human nature is that people frequently be-grudge the success of others. Regrettably, we would rather see people fail than succeed—not so much because we are bad or misguided, but because *we* would rather be the recipient of that success.

Come on, admit it! When you read about someone who has had a windfall, or won the lottery, you probably said to your friends, "Good for them, aren't they fortunate!" when inside you are really thinking, "Why them? Why not me?" Don't feel bad about it. Most of us feel the same way. We are not wicked or evil, we just want our place in the sun. Take heart and go ahead and congratulate that lucky SOB because we *will* have our day and we won't need luck to get it. The good news is that we aren't going to wait around for Lady Luck to strike; we are going to create our own breaks.

Competition is the Better Part of Valour

Remember, when we make our "Declaration of Success," we're going to generate a certain amount of conflict. Having made our declaration, we have to expect a certain amount of resistance from others around us who do not see any immediate personal benefit from our actions. This conflict may present itself in a number of different forms. It may appear in the form of natural competition, which is generally healthy. However, it may take on a more serious form due to the envy or fear created because it is perceived that you are threatening someone's position.

We must be prepared to respond to this conflict in the appro-priate manner. We must be very cautious however, because the right measure and the correct timing for the response is critical when dealing with competition and envy from coworkers. Sometimes the best response is no response—a matter of staying true to your con-victions about becoming successful. Or take a position of "He who laughs last, laughs best." Remember, as our efforts take us up the ladder, in time we may become the supervisor or manager of some of our current coworkers. We will need their cooperation even more in the future than we do today. Therefore, it will not pay to use the Vikings' slash-and-burn tactics today on those who may be our subordinates tomorrow.

Rather than fighting with envious coworkers, let's make this competition work for us. This resistance can actually be used to our advantage. Scepticism and envy are great motivators that can provide us with yet another incentive to prevail in our efforts. The main objective is to not let the negativity or resistance hold us back from moving ahead. We don't need to apologize for being ambitious. There is a big difference between being ambitious and being a heartless villain. We certainly have a conscience; but if we have to put ourselves in front of others to succeed, we must and we will. Given the choice, we will take victory rather than being counted among the "working wounded" every time.

NOTEWORTHY SAYS:

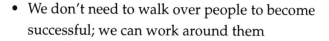

- We don't need to walk over people to become successful; we can work around them

- Be prepared for conflict when you make your "Declaration of Success"

- Keep ambition and compassion in perspective

- Today's detractors may become tomorrow's customers or subordinates

∞ **8** ∞

EROGENOUS ZONES

In an earlier chapter, the need to focus on the right people in the organization was discussed. Now let's consider the need to concentrate on the right tasks in our job. We must prioritize the areas that will yield the maximum return on our investment in our success. Through helping the organization become more efficient, increasing productivity and building the morale of our coworkers through example, we will advance. To promote and ensure that advancement, we must carefully analyze our job and identify the key areas that I call *erogenous zones*. I refer to them as erogenous zones because when these areas are stimulated, they are the most likely to move both the organization and our personal position forward. Every company has erogenous zones, the challenge is to locate these areas and get working on them.

Rather than spending an inordinate amount of time in the "dead" zones, doing the mundane chores that anyone can do, we must make time to locate and stimulate the erogenous zones. These are the areas that will produce impressive results and provide the recognition we need to move up the ladder. This is not to say that we should refuse to do any "grunt" work whatsoever. A certain amount of "grunt" comes with every job, but as time is our most valuable resource, we must be careful to allocate it wisely. The more adept we become at managing our time, the easier it will be to steer clear of the "grunt" work and focus on the glamorous, dynamic erogenous zones.

Is this self-serving? No! This is *self-rewarding.* To serve your employer to the best of your ability is good, but to both accomplish it and gain recognition for it is *great!* No employer worth working for will disagree with this formula, so start looking for the erogenous zones where you work. Find them and begin to stimulate them!

Time Waits for No One

Tick-tock, tick-tock, the grains of sand pour inexorably through the hourglass. As much as we might want, there is no stopping it. Although we cannot stop time, we must take control of our workload and manage our time effectively. Unproductive use of employees' time is one of the most common reasons that companies lose their competitive edge. How can we deal with this issue?

The first thing to do is make a list of your principal, key job responsibilities. Make this list on a separate sheet and mark it the "A" list. Then make a list of the secondary tasks (including "grunt" work) that your job entails on a second sheet and mark it the "B" list. Go back to the "A" list and examine it closely and look for those erogenous zones mentioned earlier. Arrange the list, placing these at the top. Then look at the job functions (on the "A" list) and arrange them accordingly from most important to least important.

Put both lists in a file and put them away. Now go out and buy yourself a stopwatch at the everything-for-a-dollar store.

Here are examples of an "A" list and a "B" list:

"A"

Interaction with Supervisors

Presentations to Management and Staff

Analysis of Work Areas to Determine Efficiency Levels

Developing Ways for the Organization to Increase Revenue

Developing Ways for the Organization to Increase Profit Margins

Developing Ways for the Organization to Reduce Costs

Participation in Company Training

"B"

Paperwork

Correspondence

Organization of Files

Follow-Up Calls

Studying Technical Information

The next day, when you arrive at work, get ready to make another list. On this list, you are going to track exactly where you are spending your time. On your list you are going to record the amount of time of each activity you allocated your time to throughout an *entire day*. It will be inconvenient, but this exercise will yield some amazing results. List the time allotments into different categories such as:

Meetings

On the Phone—Business

Talking to Coworkers

On the Phone—Personal

Working on Computer

Correspondence

Once you have completed this exercise, pull out your "A" and "B" lists. Now let's find out which categories you are spending your time on. After doing this, certain things will become clear very quickly. You are most likely wasting a lot of time in nonproductive areas. You would probably be better off turning your mind to mush watching situation comedies on TV! Remember, if you are going to spend the majority of your waking hours at work, let's get something out of those hours!

After you recover from the shock of wasting so much of your precious time, we are going to focus on improving our time management skills. Now go back to the "A" and "B" lists. Examine them again, this time with the objective of trying to move as many items as possible from the "A" list to the "B" list. Try to get down to no more than three different critical facets of your job. Only three, and make sure that these include at least one erogenous zone that will move both the organization and your position forward.

For the next week, rearrange everything possible so that you can concentrate as much as you can on these three areas only. Over the next three weeks, slowly start introducing up to three new facets (no more) to your schedule. After one month, review your progress in those areas and compare them to your accomplishments of the previous few months and see how they rate. Now pull out those lists again and review the "B" list. How important were those niggly little things anyway? Did your job collapse as a result of deferring them? Can you defer them further without consequence, in fact to your benefit?

As the last step in the exercise, bring your stopwatch in to work the first day after completing the exercise and do another assessment of how much time is spent in which area. Now compare that to the assessment you took just one short month ago. Needless to say, you will find the results surprising. This is a great way to discover exactly what productivity levels you are functioning on at any given time. You should find this exercise very useful, and I recommend utilizing it at least three times per year, every year.

NOTE of caution! When embarking on this time management program, be sure to use common sense. Don't neglect any areas of job performance expected of you just because they are not "erogenous zones." The operative phrase in the exercise is "to arrange everything possible" to allow time to concentrate on the important things. I don't want students of my system to be standing in the unemployment line with some dog-eared lists marked "A" and "B," waiting to explain how the time management system works to some unemployment counsellor. Use your head on this one!

The Eight-Ball

Staying in Front of the Eight-Ball

As we are evaluating and reevaluating our priorities at work, one of the biggest frustrations that will arise will be the seemingly inescapable little "warts" in our job that forever keep us from working on those critical erogenous zones. After our exercise with the lists, we should be rethinking how necessary many of these little warts are. Where possible, delegate. Try to pass those darn warts on to someone else. If you are not in a position to delegate, defer these chores. If you can't get away from them, they will follow you wherever you go until they have consumed your entire day. You will go home no further ahead than you were the previous day and, worse yet, they will be eagerly awaiting you tomorrow and the next day in even greater numbers until you are destined to spend your working life completely eclipsed by the eight-ball.

The eight-ball is a huge black orb capable of blocking out all light of hope for being productive, inspired or brilliant in any way. The black eight-ball can cast such a shadow over our career that it is comparable to being on the dark side of the moon where no life can survive, not even the smallest embryo of a creative idea. As it is progressive in nature, the further we fall under the shadow of the eight-ball, the more difficult it becomes to get out from behind it. The best strategy to deal with this is to do everything possible to avoid getting behind it in the first place.

However, as this is not always possible, we must struggle to maintain *objectivity* about our work flow so we can avoid the big black orb. Objectivity can be a saviour in times of crisis, when the brush fires are being fanned and things are beginning to spiral out of control. At that point we must completely stop everything. If possible, leave the building for five minutes, even hide in the wash-room for a few minutes and allow yourself to gain the necessary composure.

Breathe slowly and deeply and remember why you are doing this job in the first place. Recall the master plan and remind yourself that you are in control. True, you came close to allowing events to begin controlling you, but you put your foot down and broke the momentum that was building against you and you are now regaining control. You will march back to your work, stop the flow of incoming information and systematically attack each problem, beginning at the most relevant to the crisis and work your way down the list. As soon as you assume this mind set, you are on the way to winning, because you are now in the process of controlling events as opposed to the events controlling you. This is what *objectivity* can do for you.

As we discovered in our exercise with the lists, it requires a daily, focused effort to avoid having your time absorbed in nonproductive activities. We must resist the temptation to be dragged behind the eight-ball and spending any significant amount of time there. Stay focused and stick to your list!

Sometimes Less is More

We've all heard the old saying, "Don't work hard, work smart." I'm going to take it one step farther and tell you that the most effective way of dealing with some tasks is by *doing little or nothing at all.* Believe it or not, some people have been extremely successful and have built entire careers based on only one or two great ideas. The key is to be able to make the time to come up with those ideas and put them into action. As we discussed earlier, one idea can lead to another until something brilliant evolves. Brilliant moves can come in the most unusual forms at the most unexpected times and may even come about by doing absolutely nothing at all.

The first time I was exposed to this concept was when I was about seventeen years old and I was hired to play one of my first one-nighters as a musician. These are interesting and challenging jobs, because you sometimes play with other musicians you have never met before, and you have no idea what songs you will be asked to play. How I was referred to this band leader I'll never know, because I was a very green musician and I didn't know many songs.

I was hired by a raving alcoholic named Bud who drank himself to death, but before he did, he managed to become a pretty good piano player. As I had recently joined the musician's union, my name was on a roster of available players and I guess old Bud just looked down the list and stopped at my name. The job was in a smoky lounge with elastic terry cloth table tops, purple shag carpet and one of those sparkling mirrored disco globes hanging above the dance floor.

Fortunately he started the first set with a song I knew and I was able to make my way through without a hitch. The next series of songs however, were not so easy and consisted of titles that I had never heard of, let alone played before! Was this to be the deciding moment when the wicked old piano teacher would have her revenge for me daring to make a living as a musician? Never!

Bud called the next tune and looked over at me through his bloodshot eyes. His face, one that showed many years of alcohol abuse, smiled wryly, as he was about to take me on an embarrassing ride through a tune that I couldn't have carried if it had handles. He counted one, two, three, four. At the end of that count I was to meet my destiny. I was afraid that my career would end that night, fearful that Bud might even take my ignorance personally and think I was trying to make him sound bad. I clearly saw the crossroads in front of me.

It would take months to learn all of the songs he had up his sleeve for me that night but I only had seconds to respond. Although the audience consisted primarily of half-gassed street people, prostitutes and junkies, I still had my pride. It was time to take control of the situation instead of the situation controlling me. It was time to come up with some brilliant moves, it was time to make less become more!

As the drummer and bass player began the intro, I stepped forward and faced the crowd. Bud placed his hands firmly on the keys and I made my move. I quickly turned off the volume on my guitar and began stroking away at the strings and moving my hands around the neck of my guitar with total confidence. I looked at Bud with a big smile on my face and the song sounded great all the way through. Fortunately, there were only a few solo parts for me, at which time I cranked up the volume and played a very short burst of notes in the neighbourhood of the key the song was in and managed to get away with it the entire evening.

During the break at the end of the first set, Bud came over to me and pushed that mass of broken blood veins around his nose right up into my face and said, "You are the mellowest guitar player I ever played with. Every guitar player in town plays way too loud, but you're great, nice and quiet." As it was, that technique squeaked me through more than one sticky situation in my musical career and is an example of what we might use when confronted by desperate situations.

Needless to say, it is better to be prepared than to have to "fake it." But if we are faced with overwhelming odds, sometimes the most brilliant move you can make is no move at all. Remember, even Einstein wasn't a genius twenty-four hours a day!

NOTEWORTHY SAYS:

- Prioritize work areas that will yield results, the erogenous zones

- Stay in front of the eight-ball

- Maintain objectivity when events begin controlling you

- When in doubt, less is more

∞ **9** ∞

CLIMBING THE MOUNTAIN

To gain another perspective on our situation, let's put our efforts to meet the challenges of loving our job on hold for a moment. Let's travel to another time and another world, a world very similar to the one we live in today. Let's consider the story of a brave young person who encounters some of the problems that we face in getting, keeping and loving a good job in our world.

This is the story of a young lad named Ned. His given name was Edward, but because he was a small fellow and somewhat prone to clumsiness, he was affectionately known by his "friends" as Ned the "Nerd." Although he was a bright young man with considerable potential, he had accepted the title of "nerd" during his early days at school. Unfortunately, it stuck to him with the tenacity of a tattoo and seemed impossible to outgrow.

Ned and his mother lived in a small village in the shadow of the Big Mountain. Ned had only a faint recollection of the father who had left him and his mother when he was just a tyke. As the two of them had to fend for themselves, his mother worked very hard, taking in the neighbours' laundry and doing piecework as a seamstress.

As the head of a single-parent household, life for Ned's mother was hard, but through the drudgery shone her dream of saving enough money to send Ned away to the prestigious university on the other side of the Big Mountain. Because of their limited income, Ned was barely able to finish public school, let alone go on to obtain a degree from an institution of higher learning.

Ned had a part-time job while he was attending school and, at this point, he considered himself lucky to have developed it into a full-time job after he graduated. He worked as a mortician's assistant at the funeral home at the end of town. Not a glamorous job, but work was steady and the pay was decent. It had its shortcomings just like any job might, but aside from having his "friends" (who called him "Nerd") bug him about it being a "dead"-end job, it really wasn't so bad. Besides, he had the responsibility of supplementing his mother's meagre income, so it would have to do for now.

Ned was responsible for "making up" the deceased in preparation for viewing by their families at the funeral. Although he had a minimal amount of personal interaction with the people he met at work, he took pride in making them look their best for what would be their last public appearance. He was sure that they appreciated his work as well, even though it was difficult for them to show their gratitude.

Ned worked away each day making his clients look their very best, with rosy cheeks and ruby lips. Ruby, at least for the female clients; he gave the males more of a flesh tone, unless of course they specifically requested ruby lips in their Last Will and Testament.

As Ned did his work on the refrigerated level of the funeral home, he was able to see out of a large window above his work station. Through the window, Ned could see the Big Mountain looming boldly in the sky. Every day as he worked, he looked off into the distance and dreamed of one day going up to the summit of the Big Mountain.

No one from the village had ever gone up the Big Mountain and come back to tell of it. The legend said that those who ventured up the Big Mountain fell to their doom on its slippery slopes. Others tales told of hapless climbers being enslaved by evil trolls that forced them to do paperwork for minimum wage. Either way, the villagers would have no part of climbing the Big Mountain.

Their fear was so great that when the people sent their sons and daughters away to the prestigious university on the other side of the Big Mountain, they were required to undertake an arduous journey all the way around it—a journey so rigorous that many could not complete it.

Some were felled by bandits. Others got married and had children along the way and had to get jobs before they could reach their destination. A difficult journey indeed, but as an alternative to going over the Big Mountain, the people of the village accepted it as the way of their world and rarely questioned it.

Occasionally, some hot shot with designer hiking boots would challenge the Big Mountain, and trek off into its misty foothills with morbid spectators cheering him on. As time went on, even the spectators were few and far between. There was nothing more to see than the backs of some poor victims who didn't know any better.

Each time a crowd gathered at the bottom of the Big Mountain to christen another journey and wait for the return of the adventurers, nothing became of it. No one ever returned. The only thing remaining of the daring journeys were tales of gruesome endings for those who dared to scale the Big Mountain.

As he was growing up in the shadow of the Big Mountain, Ned was never afraid of it like the other villagers were. Although he never mentioned it to anyone, he was fascinated by it and secretly believed that his destiny was somehow tied to the Big Mountain. Even so, he would not go near it, much less discuss it, for fear of upsetting his fragile mother. The only discussion of the Big Mountain that Ned's mother was interested in was how Ned was going to get around it one day on his way to the prestigious university on the other side.

Things in the village went along without event as one day passed to the next. Ned made his clients' cheeks rosy and their lips ruby (unless it specified otherwise in their Last Will and Testament), and everything was as it should be when suddenly his boss came running into the refrigerated level of the funeral home where Ned was working.

"Ned! We're in trouble! We've got three burials coming up this weekend and somebody screwed up on the order for the floral arrangements. We've got three requests for lilacs, and every florist in town has them on back order. What will we do?!"

It was unusual for his boss to discuss floral arrangements or other areas of the business with Ned, so he must have been in a real bind over this. Being the helpful sort that he was, Ned quickly thought of something and offered it up to his boss.

"I know of a place at the foot of the Big Mountain where lilacs used to grow wild. I think it was about this time of year that I remember seeing them."

"Are you sure?" asked his boss.

"Pretty sure. What's the alternative?" replied Ned.

"Look Ned. I can't go near the Big Mountain. My wife would kill me and I'm not really sure where this place is that you're talking about. Can you do me a major favour and go up there and see if you can get some for us? There'll be a bonus in it for you," implored his boss.

Ned's boss had come running into the refrigerated level of the funeral home in such a tizzy, he had unintentionally left the door open as he entered. As he was explaining the situation to Ned, the warm air had been flowing in on the client that Ned had been making up. While Ned was calculating whether he would be able to finish with his client and get to the base of the Big Mountain and back before dark, the ruby lips of his client began to twitch from the contact with the warm air. It was as though Ned was getting some encouragement from beyond the mortal world as his client seemed to smile at the prospect of him taking on this assignment.

"Okay. I'll try to bail you out on this one. But you'd better close the door or I'll have to do this client over again; he's starting to sweat."

Ned quickly finished up his job and got ready to head out to the foothills of the Big Mountain. He could hardly contain his excitement and hoped that nothing would happen to change his boss's mind before he left. If his mother knew about this, it would be all over. There would be no way she would sanction the journey.

It was late afternoon as Ned headed toward the end of town and up the path that would take him to where he had seen those wild lilacs a few seasons ago. He bristled with excitement as the wind blew through his hair; he had this strange sensation that, somehow, he was embarking on an adventure that would propel him to the destiny that he had dreamed of all his life.

As he travelled up the winding path, the Big Mountain stood before him as he had never seen it before. Grand and omnipotent, it stretched into the sky as its slopes disappeared into the clouds far above the ground where Ned stood. On this day, so overwhelming was the Big Mountain that Ned felt compelled to kneel down and acknowledge its splendour, to pay tribute to its unknown powers.

Ned got up and walked down the embankment where he remembered the field of lilacs lay. Sure enough, there it was. Right before his eyes was the solution to his boss's problem and the doorway to the bonus he had been promised. As the sun was edging its way lower in the sky, Ned hurried to gather up his lilacs and head back down the trail in order to reach the village before dark.

He eagerly collected enough for the three ceremonies as well as for two more, just in case any unexpected clients were dropped at work before the back orders at the florist were filled. As he was wrapping them up in a nice neat bundle to take them back home, Ned saw a strange light up at the end of the path that led up the through the foothills.

He had never seen anything quite like it and, being a curious young lad, he put down his bundle of lilacs and headed up the path toward the mysterious light. As he came to the end of the path where the rocky base of the mountain began in earnest, the light was much further up the hill than it had originally appeared to be. Not to be put off, Ned began scaling the craggy slope one rock at a time and pursued the elusive, flickering light.

On and on Ned climbed until finally he came to a large flat rock that sat at the end of a trail that wound its way gently up the side of the Big Mountain. Although Ned had never been anywhere near here before—in fact he had never known anyone from the village who had ventured this far up the Big Mountain—he was determined to find the source of the light he saw up ahead. He was going to have to move fast though, because the daylight was starting to fade and he had to return home before dark or his mother would be very worried.

He followed the path as it wound around and around. As soon as he thought he was getting close to reaching the light, it would appear farther away. Then suddenly, it disappeared! The light was gone! And in his search for it, going up and down the paths, he wasn't sure exactly where he was. In fact, as he turned to head back down, each direction looked the same now. Ned was lost! Not only was he lost, even if he knew which way to go, he would only be able to walk for a few more minutes before it would be too dark to see where he was going.

Night was upon him and Ned was *lost on the Big Mountain!* Where scores of villagers had fallen to their death. Where evil trolls forced their victims to perform unspeakable acts. And he had left the lilacs back in the glen, which defeated the original purpose of his journey. Good one, Ned!

It was dark now, and it became cool as the moon rose in the sky and Ned was very frightened. He wrapped his coat around him very tightly and, huddled by the trunk of a huge tree, he began to think about his life back home. He wondered if his mother had contacted his boss by now. And what would she say to him when she found out that he had gone up to the Big Mountain by himself and hadn't returned after nightfall?

His miserable thoughts were interrupted by a rustling noise coming from the bushes down the pathway. Ned's thoughts, along with his stomach, began churning anew, this time with visions of trolls ten feet tall, with long hairy arms and large claws on each hand. The rustling became louder as his visions heightened into a crescendo of terror.

His fear climaxed when out of the thicket, not more than a few feet in front of him, a large, hairy creature stepped out into the moonlight. It must have been seven feet tall, with big twisty ears and a large, pointed nose. Its shining eyes peered down its long nose and focused directly on Ned. Ned was face-to-face with a troll!

Ned let out a great cry as he felt two powerful claws clutch his arms from behind him. It was another troll. This one was as large and hairy as the first, and because of its close proximity to Ned, he became aware of a very strong stench coming from the beast. The smell intensified and he felt a raspy cloth rub over his head and down his shoulders as the powerful creature behind him slipped Ned into a burlap bag as though he was a bundle of firewood.

"Bring him," said the first troll—the one who had stood in front of Ned moments ago. They headed off into the forest and up the steep slopes of the Big Mountain. On and on they climbed. The trolls travelled quickly and silently into the night with Ned bouncing around in that smelly sack for what seemed like hours. Finally they stopped just inside a huge cavern near the top of the Big Mountain.

Ned was dropped out of the sack onto the floor of the huge cave, and around him stood at least a dozen of these hairy creatures, all peering down their long noses at Ned's trembling little body. This was the lair of the trolls! Since he was a little boy, Ned had always dreamed of climbing the Big Mountain, but he never imagined that the mountain had this in store for him.

Several of the trolls stepped aside and behind them, sitting on the massive head of a tree stump carved into a throne, was the biggest, hairiest one of them all, the King of the Trolls!

He pointed a bony finger down at Ned and asked "Why have you come to my mountain?"

Frozen with fear, young Ned could only mumble in reply, "I, I, uhhhh...."

The words of the King of the Trolls rolled out like thunder as he repeated his question, "Why, boy, have you come onto my Mountain?!"

Ned regained his composure and whimpered, "For lilacs, sir, lilacs."

"Lilacs?" snorted the king. "Where are they, then?"

Ned began to find his confidence, primarily based on the fact that he was actually in a conversation with the Troll King discussing the issues, as opposed to being skinned alive and roasted as an appetizer for his subjects. He bravely told his story, right from the beginning, as the great Troll King listened intently, without expression.

After Ned told his story, the King sat silently for many minutes and seemed to consider very carefully what Ned had said. He finally shifted on his throne and asked, "Why do your people have such a fascination with my mountain? They come here year after year and trespass on my land and trample my bushes and leave their garbage behind. Why?"

Ned explained that most of the people meant well and were simply looking for an easier way to reach the prestigious university in the village on the other side of the Big Mountain.

Again the King sat motionlessly as he carefully considered the information that Ned had given him. "I wouldn't mind so much if your people weren't so destructive. Their attitude has put me in a very bad mood for many years. And now a great tragedy has visited me, and my mood is even more sour. As long as I feel this way, no one shall pass over my mountain!" the King roared.

"What tragedy, sir?" asked Ned.

The King began to tell the story of how his only son had become stricken with a sickness. He had developed a very high fever from which he eventually died. This had happened only three days ago, and the King was deeply disturbed by these events. Worse still, the trolls were unable to bury his son, their Prince, because his face was left with a tortured expression when he died from the fever. As was the custom with the trolls, they would not, they could not, bury their kind without a peaceful expression on their face. The trolls believed that the expression that you were buried with would dictate the course of your afterlife, and those left with disturbed expressions would be unsettled forever in the next world.

The King was very sad as he told the story and began to weep as he concluded the telling of it.

Then Ned got an idea. He said "Don't cry, Great King, I can help."

The King stopped instantly and looked with anger at Ned and replied, "You? A puny villager who couldn't even find his way down my mountain?"

"Yes, me," Ned said firmly.

Ned told the King and his subjects that he had been an apprentice to a mortician since his early school days and that if he was given the chance, he could restore the young prince's expression to its earlier state and make it possible for the trolls to bury him and remain true to their beliefs.

The King was amazed by this suggestion and sat for many minutes contemplating what young Ned had proposed. He finally broke his silence and replied, "Young man, if you can do what you claim you can, I will have my trolls take you safely back to the foothills and set you free to return to your life."

Ned stepped forward and stood as tall as he could and looked directly into the eyes of the King and said, "If I can do as I claim, not only will you set me free, you must grant passage for me and the people of my village to cross your lands and travel over your mountain at our will, for the rest of time!"

The King stood upright in shock and the other trolls began to close the circle around Ned, and all of them began to smell very bad. He took three steps toward Ned and said, "If you do as you say you can, I will grant your request of access to my mountain by the people of your village, but only if they are accompanied by you. You are a brave young man to make such a request and if you are capable of what you claim, you will deserve it. If you are not, I will roast you and eat you and that will be the end of that!"

He stepped forward and grabbed Ned by the arm and said "On to my son's resting place! We will soon have a burial, or a snack! One or the other. Come, everyone!"

Ned was led deep into the cave with the other trolls following. He was filled with undiluted adrenaline at this point, and he knew he was truly facing a do-or-die situation. They soon arrived at the burial site, situated by a large, dark subterranean pool. The King's son lay wrapped in cloth at the end of the pathway at the very edge of the pool. The King sat Ned down beside his son and said, "Let's see what you are all about, boy."

As Ned began to inspect the Prince's condition, he noticed that the other trolls were laying a fire and beginning to fashion a spit capable of roasting a fairly large meal. This gave little comfort to Ned, but he bravely told the King, "I'll need some things from the forest: roots, herbs and oils from the trees that I will describe to you."

The King looked at his son, then looked over at the barbecue his trolls were preparing and said, "Very well, but you haven't much time. All this talk has made my trolls hungry."

Ned began preparing the Prince; when the items he requested arrived, he went to work in earnest. Miraculously, as soon as he began his treatment, the muscles in the Prince's face began to relax and his face was quickly restored to a more peaceful countenance.

"I can give him rosy cheeks and ruby lips as well, if you like." Ned said cheerily to the king.

"No thanks, he is fine the way you have made him. Absolutely amazing!"

The King's mood quickly transformed into one of joy. All of his trolls were very happy, too, because when the King was happy, everybody was happy. It had been a long time since the King was this happy—since before the village came to be at the bottom of his mountain.

"You've done it, lad!" proclaimed the King. "Put away the firewood," he called out to his trolls, "and prepare to honour our end of the bargain by taking him back to his people."

The trolls escorted Ned back down the mountain and, just as dawn was beginning to break, they reached the foothills of the Big Mountain. The King and the trolls bid Ned farewell and explained to him that he would always be welcome on the mountain, as would the other villagers providing they were accompanied by Ned, as the terms of the agreement stipulated.

As he came out of the foothills, Ned saw an encampment of villagers who had been out looking for him the night before. He called out to them as he emerged from the foothills and they came rushing up to greet him. Among them was his mother, who cried for joy at the sight of seeing her only son alive and well after spending the night on the Big Mountain.

"Are you all right, Ned?" she asked.

"I'm fine, Mother," he replied. "I've had a great adventure and I've tamed the Big Mountain once and for all!" cried Ned.

"You better come back to the village and tell us all about it," said his mother.

Ned returned back to the village a hero, as he was the only villager to have gone up the Big Mountain and returned to tell of it. With his new popularity, everyone in the village now included in their Last Will and Testament a request for Ned to do the makeup for their last public appearance. As flattering as this was to Ned, he retired from his job at the funeral home and became the highest paid person in the village. He became the village's only tour guide of the Big Mountain and could charge whatever he wanted to take people over the mountain or to bring them back from the other side.

Ned later married, and he and his wife lived happily ever after. Ned's mother was the proudest mother in the village, due to her son's great success. Her dream of Ned going to the prestigious university on the other side came true as well. Although he never attended the university, he visited it many times on his highly paid tours from the other side of the mountain.

And after his adventure, they never called him Ned the "Nerd" again!

THE NOTEWORTHY MORAL OF THE STORY

- Never give up on your dreams

- When you have established a position of strength during negotiations ... go for the whole enchilada!

- As large as the obstacle seems, there is always a way over it or around it

- *Your* special skills and abilities may be the ones that save the day

❧ **10** ❧

UNORTHODOX WINS THE RACE

The Repeaters Versus the Originators

In a time when there is so much importance attached to being successful, we need every possible advantage we can get to make us stand out from the crowd. What can we do in order to distinguish ourselves in our job? The way to accomplish this is to begin to ask questions. Let's look at what we are doing and how we are doing it and ask ourselves the big question: *Why?*

Exactly *why* are we doing our job the way we are doing it? The answer will most likely be, "That's the way we've always done it!" Or, "That's the way we were trained to do it, and that's the way it's always been done." Naturally, some of the systems we follow at work are in place because they work effectively and probably require little in the way of refinement. However, upon closer examination you will probably find that there are many inherent problems within certain systems. Problems that are perpetuated by operators who have made the same mistakes over and over because they were *trained to perpetuate those problems!*

Incredible, but true. In order to understand this situation we have to become as objective as possible and get to the heart of the issue, which is: *We live in a world of repeaters.* Repeaters—passers of information that goes from one person to the next, regurgitated over and over as unchallenged fact when, in reality, much of that information is *incorrect!* This is more pronounced than ever today because technology is evolving so quickly that very few of us can get a grip on it. Consequently, there are many self-proclaimed experts generating incomplete or inaccurate information that is in turn passed on by the next repeater.

How is this possible?! It is not only possible, it is a chilling reality. We are by nature, instinctively repeaters. We follow patterns and habits without question, just like many of the other species with whom we share the Earth. A dog turns in a circle several times before it lays down to sleep, a spider spins its web in a certain design every time without fail, a robin builds its nest in the same way over and over without question. In the same way, many employees unintentionally repeat the same mistakes over and over again.

Wait a minute! We are the superior species on the planet, we have the technology, we have the intelligence to reason. But do we use that reason as often as we might, or are we satisfied to repeat our actions habitually because "If it ain't broke don't fix it"? We are naturally drawn to be repeaters because we are trained to do so at a very early age.

Right from the beginning we are told things that we happily consume as gospel. We implicitly trust our sources of information—our parents and our teachers, even Dan Rather. Of course they love us (our parents probably, our teachers maybe and Dan I don't know about) and have no reason to steer us in the wrong direction; but if the information they are passing along is inaccurate or incomplete, we still end up with misinformation.

Nowhere is this condition more prevalent than in today's workplace. Most companies are modeled after other companies, and as most businesses are not created out of a textbook or in a test tube, they do not always adhere to precise formulas. Owners and managers have had to adapt to economic conditions and the desires of consumers as they fluctuate over the years. As certain systems and procedures have been modified to respond to those fluctuations, various glitches and gremlins have occurred that have ingrained themselves into those systems and have become innocently but habitually repeated over time.

Amazingly enough, all of this actually presents enormous opportunities for analytical employees, because distinction, acknowledgment and advancement await those who can refine and improve systems and get those gremlins packing. So how do we capitalize on these opportunities?

By asking questions, questions, and more questions. Reevaluate what you are told about anything and everything! Who is the author of the information? Where did they get *their* information? Are they the actual author of the information or simply a repeater of someone else's diluted or inaccurate message? Are they sharing genuine knowledge, or are they slanting information to protect a hidden agenda or a vested interest? Have yesterday's solutions become today's problems?

As soon as you begin to ask these questions and to analyze things more closely, you will quickly realize that there is very little original, first-generation information around. You will discover that at least 90 percent of the people we deal with in our jobs are repeaters! Of course we can't expect everyone to be gushing with original ideas like Bill Gates or Thomas Edison, but once we have this realization, we can immediately see the importance of having accurate information and the value of original ideas. We can also see the value in challenging ourselves to break out of the cycle of repetition and trying to come up with something original.

There are, of course, many levels to developing original ideas. There is something called "parallel creativity," where two parties come up with the same conclusion or discovery at similar times, entirely independent of one another. And there is the process of elimination, where after trying all the ideas that don't work, we are left with the one that does. And for those of us void of ethics, you can descend into the lowest level of creativity and practise plagiarism and outright pirating of others' original ideas.

This doesn't mean that ideas should not be shared or duplicated. In fact, virtually all ideas are variations or extensions of existing ones. There is no ownership or copyright of ideas. But if we become reliant on repeating the ideas of others, we will stunt our creative growth and limit our potential to develop our own original ideas. Furthermore, in duplicating others' ideas and systems, we may inherit the gremlins that are part of those ideas and systems. Or we could end up building our idea on a shaky foundation of misinformation collected from *repeaters* or other self-proclaimed experts.

If we carefully consider these possibilities, there may be nothing wrong with borrowing ideas and making original modifications or extensions to them. But we still need to develop our creativity and our ability to become original. This might simply involve taking something basic, something obvious, and improving it and putting our own slant on it. We may not have to reinvent the wheel, but you will be amazed at what you can come up with by looking at something old and taking a new, *unorthodox* approach to it. (Refer back to Chapter Three, "Creativity at Work.")

NOTE of caution here: Being unorthodox involves taking risks. Our unorthodox ideas risk rejection and we take the chance of appearing to "rock the boat." We've touched on dealing with rejection in an earlier chapter so let's look at how to deal with "rocking the boat." This can be done by addressing the development, packaging and marketing of our ideas.

Product Development

In this instance, our product is our idea and we must go to great lengths to ensure that our product is well thought out and carefully considered before we present it. Employers are always interested in new ideas that can move their business forward. However, you must carefully and thoroughly research your idea first to make sure it is indeed an improvement over what is presently being done and that it will be a net benefit to the organization.

Packaging

Just as all successful major corporations take great pains to package their products provocatively, we must give the same attention to the packaging of our product, our idea. Our packaging will be the *presentation* of our idea; it must be clear, concise and powerful enough to carry our idea through any initial resistance that might be encountered. In the development of our presentation, we must also factor in the possibility that people's egos may be at stake when new ways to approach old problems are presented. It may be *your* supervisor who is directly responsible for introducing the gremlins into the system that you are about to overhaul. Be absolutely sure that you have accounted for this in your presentation and take the necessary steps to avoid making someone else (particularly a manager or supervisor) look bad.

If you have addressed this last issue, and you have developed a solid presentation, you will have created a no-lose scenario because your supervisors will acknowledge and respect the fact that you have shown the initiative to try to improve the organization. If they buy into your idea and it works, you will end up as a hero and achieve the desired distinction that your unorthodox approach will have generated.

Marketing

Again, just as the successful major corporations carefully develop their products and give great attention to their packaging, they spend a lot of time developing a marketing plan for those products. Just as they do, *we* must carefully develop a plan to market our product. Our idea must be presented in a powerful fashion with an unorthodox "hook" in it to create the necessary level of attention. Here's an example of an unorthodox "hook" that once helped me get my message across in spades.

When I was elected president of the Association of Private Career Trainers, I had a number of unconventional ideas I needed to sell to a diverse group of directors and members. At the first meeting of my presidency, I arranged to have, on cue, a woman dressed in a full Highland costume enter the room playing the bagpipes. Because it was so unexpected and yes, unorthodox to have an event like this occur at a business meeting, it brought the house down!

To this day, that event will go down in the history of the Association as being one of the most memorable ever. Needless to say, it softened up the members and made my nonconforming ideas that much easier to sell.

The Piper in Full Highland Costume

An important part of marketing any product is timing, so not only will you need to have a strong product with the right packaging, it must be presented at the correct time to have the desired impact. When I brought in the bagpiper, I didn't do it just before the people went home, I didn't start out with it, I waited until all the introductions were done and everyone was settled in, and Wham!

I gave it to them right between the eyes as the piper came marching in with the bags a'wailing.

When it comes to presenting your idea, only you will know when the best time for the delivery will be. Use common sense and assess all the variables, the personalities, and the protocol involved. Calculate the precise moment to drop the bomb into their laps so it will be the most unexpected and the most appreciated.

Never Cry Wolf

When you are being unorthodox, you may find yourself swimming against the current in your job. This comes with the territory, and a certain degree of resistance to new ideas should be expected. However, even though we are always looking for ways to improve and to advance, we must be careful not to be perceived as overdoing it. If your ideas are generally good and well received, you can always get away with one or two flops. But don't come out with anything half-baked and don't oversaturate the management with your ideas. Part of the finesse of timing is knowing when to avoid attracting attention to yourself.

NOTEWORTHY SAYS:

- People have a tendency to be repeaters, rather than originators of ideas and information

- Always question the source and the accuracy of information

- Unorthodox approaches can yield original ideas and solutions

- Focus on the development, packaging and marketing of your ideas

- Never cry wolf! Know when to avoid attracting attention

ᙢ 11 ᙢ

LOVE IT OR LEAVE IT

Educating Your Employer

Now that we have learned ways to improve our situation at work, it is time to consider one of the final steps in the process of loving our job—to educate your employer. Traditionally, the relationship between employers and employees has been hierarchical in nature. The roles were clearly defined as boss and worker, leader and follower, lord and peasant. Knowledge and information travelled in one direction, from the top downward.

Fortunately, today the emphasis is shifting to a more team-oriented environment. In many jobs there are "coaches" or "facilitators" rather than bosses. However, many companies and organizations are in varying stages of this transition and the more progressive ones are still in the minority. Just because we are aware of the importance of developing and utilizing the ideas and skills discussed earlier, this doesn't mean that our supervisors and employers necessarily have the same awareness.

I have been fortunate to have the opportunity to work with some brilliant people throughout my career. I have also worked with my share of ignorant people. If you are in the position of working for one of the less brilliant, it does not have to get in the way of your personal progress and it may actually present some opportunities; it always has for me.

Regarding ignorance—it can be found in abundance throughout the world. Although you may feel that *your* supervisors and coworkers are particularly endowed in this area, the day that you begin to over-assess their weaknesses is the day you begin a downward spiral in the opposite direction of progress. As overwhelming as the temptation may be, avoid measuring your employers. Our first concern is not how great our employers or our coworkers are, it is how great *we can become.* But by improving the awareness level of our employers, we can improve our relationship with them and be much more successful under their employ.

Our objective is to influence the behaviour of our managers, primarily in areas where it affects us directly, by making sure they know what a great job we are doing and how much they depend on us. Another area we can influence that will affect us indirectly is the attitude of the organization toward the quality of products it produces. Sometimes the most powerful people in an organization, the ones who stand to benefit the most by serving their customers, can lose sight of the significance of this issue. You may have more influence in this area than you think and you must assume responsibility for helping your employers stay in touch with this fundamental concept. Any organization that doesn't listen to the needs of its customers is going to be toasted, roasted and flambéd! In subtle ways, try to help the boss remember that the customer is always right. As long as you promote this credo, you will always be right, too.

Monkey Do, Monkey Don't See

To understand them better (refer back to the "Wizard of Oz Syndrome" in Chapter Four, "Power to the Communicators"), remember that although our employers have a certain degree of control over our livelihood, they should be considered as people first, then as benefactors. As people, they are prone to all the common types of prejudices and narrow thinking that can befall any of us. Therefore we must extend compassion and tolerance toward them, just as we hope they will toward us when we fall prey to those ever-present human shortcomings.

In being human, one of the biggest problems that face employers is that some of them have difficulty in recognizing certain accomplishments of their employees. This is not because they are incapable of doing so, it is probably because it is not in their best interest (even subconsciously) to provide that recognition. Have you ever come up with an idea that you thought was absolutely brilliant and yet the corporate "gatekeepers" in a position to promote your idea cannot seem to grasp the genius of it?

The reason for this is sometimes quite simple. It is because *they* didn't think of it! How could it be such a great idea? The second and most disturbing part of this scenario is, not only did *they not think of it, they may not be capable of coming up with an idea like that!* The denial of your idea is not malevolent in any way, it is strictly a defense mechanism to protect their ego! Certainly this may not be the case for every idea we introduce, but rejection may be waiting to greet our very best idea.

How do we respond to this? When we structure the presentation for our idea, we want to be sure to either give some credit to one of the corporate gatekeepers, or better yet, make them think that it was at least partially *their* idea. Suddenly, the recognition of and attention to your idea will take on a whole new dimension.

On the surface, if it seems that we have sold out, that is only a short-term assessment. In the long term, this tactic will get us the recognition we deserve because we will be gradually educating the gatekeepers and, if they see they can be a part of something brilliant, they may be convinced to let us share in the glory as well.

If we are going to truly love our job, one of the biggest responsibilities, and what may become our greatest achievement, will be to educate our employers. This may sound like the one thing that is most likely to get us fired. Needless to say, the process of educating your employer requires interpersonal interaction that is both subtle and sophisticated. As daring and delicate as this seems, we must take the risk because this process is a critical step in taking control of our career destiny.

Whenever I discuss the concept of educating employers, I recommend developing this skill cautiously. I always have visions of fertile imaginations coming up with all sorts of partially evolved versions of this. I see bosses all over town being faced on Monday morning by some overly zealous employees reading them the riot act. Then I see a group of those same bosses storming into my office to give me their own thoughts, somewhat like those patrons in that bar in 1972 Whitehorse!

Job Security

If it is going to be impossible to educate your employer, and the gatekeepers fail to respond to your repeated efforts, then you may have arrived at the big career crossroads in the sky. The one that says, love your job or leave your job. If you have tried absolutely everything you can to improve your situation and you just can't make it work, then it is time to address the issue of job security, or perhaps more appropriately, job insecurity.

If you are unable to thrive in your working environment, you are in the wrong place and you going to have to search for greener pastures. Although venturing into the unknown will be an adjustment, it is basically a matter of short-term pain for long-term gain. Being in a bad job is like being in a bad relationship. If you stay in it, it will erode your self-esteem and make your life miserable; and no amount of money is worth that. (Remember Chapter One, "You Call This Fun?") If you have accepted the fact that your relationship is not working, for your own self-preservation it's time to say good bye, sayonara and ciao, baby!

Job security doesn't have to be such a frightening proposition. As labour markets move toward a fee-for-service model, as discussed in the next chapter, we will have to begin thinking more about how to generate income as opposed to getting a permanent job. What this translates into is the only real job security you have—your ability to perform and to develop original ideas and concepts. And for those of us who can think for ourselves and are committed to having fun and attaining career bliss, this is a positive trend.

In the good old days of permanent jobs, a person would have one job for life. Today we are expected to have an average of *seven or more different jobs* in a lifetime. As someone who has had many careers, I can say that this is a very positive trend indeed. The diversity of places, people and situations you have the opportunity to be exposed to by having different jobs is fantastic. Furthermore, if you decide to start your own business, as a corporation or a consultant, all of those diverse experiences and skills that you pick up along the way will allow you to become that much more successful.

As a musician, job instability is a way of life. You are

usually hired on a Monday night and fired on a Saturday night. And that weekly cycle is a luxury compared to playing one-nighters. Imagine losing your job at the end of each day! Under these circumstances you have to learn to be adaptable.

I remember my very first three-night-a-week job as a musician. Because one of the member's parents knew someone who worked there, my band was hired "on spec" by one of the large local hotels. I know I wasn't sixteen yet, because I didn't have a driver's licence and my brother drove me to the job. The band sounded good the first night, and we were asked to continue working Thursdays through Saturdays on a trial basis.

The next morning my mother called me to the phone to say that some strange man was asking for me. I answered the phone and was greeted by a scary voice that must have been attached to a very large, very mean person.

"This is Fred Duck. I'm with the Musicians Union, Local 145. I understand you boys are playing down at the hotel and you're not members of the union. We don't go for that around here."

I was startled and quite frightened by this. Mr. Duck, believe it or not, then uttered the classic line, "If you don't come down here and join the union today, you'll never work in this town again!"

It may sound funny now, but I can assure you that at fifteen years of age trying to start a career as a musician, it was anything but. I immediately got on the phone and contacted the other members and explained the situation to them. Later that morning we all piled down to the union hall and each paid our $125 (a lot of money in those days) and agreed to pay the $55 yearly dues and a percentage of our wages.

At that point I learned what the expression "paying dues" really meant. The members of the band and myself had felt that joining the union was a necessary evil and as we were going to get many jobs in the future, we would recoup our investment quickly, so why not?

That afternoon, the call came in from the kid whose parents helped arrange the job for us. "Bad news. We just got fired. Now that we're in the union, we have to charge so much money to play at the hotel, they can't afford to hire us any more!"

The ironic thing was, that apart from the one night stand I got with Bud, the alcoholic piano player, that's the last union job I played in my career as a musician! This experience made a very strong impression on me about job security. Other than what you create for yourself, there is none!

There Are Other Fish in the Sea

Sometimes, what our career needs the most is a disruption, a break from being routine and safe. We may need a little push off the precipice into the unknown in order to find or create a better job. When you come to this unknown and you are not sure whether to make the move or not, remember this: *Pressure makes diamonds.* Your move could provide the additional degree of pressure that will force you to achieve more of your potential.

If it comes down to the inevitable, don't worry. Although we are experiencing a difficult job market, there are always other opportunities out there. Even if you have to settle for something a little less in the short term, find the job or offer the service that will provide you with the maximum opportunity for personal and professional growth. Just make sure you have something to go to before you leave your old job.

There are many good books available on the subject of finding a job so I won't go into detail here. However, you should know that the majority of jobs, goods jobs, are not advertised. You need to prospect, network and dig deep for these jobs, but they are definitely out there.

If you are not sure where to start looking, I strongly recommend you investigate the hotel and restaurant sectors of the service industry. This is one area that continues to expand; in some regions, tourism and hospitality are the fastest growing industries around. One of the reasons I like this area so much is because of the potential for relatively rapid advancement. Another is the training that is provided within the industry. And you don't need to have a massive academic background to break into it either. People have gone into this field with very little education or training and have ended up becoming very successful. The most important ability you require is "people skills." If you like people and you are energetic, this could be a great industry for you. It's also a great way to meet interesting people; and, if you work hard, you can basically write your own ticket.

If you can't love your current job and you are ready to move onward (and upward), remember to apply the information discussed in Chapter Six, "Networking," and become as resourceful as possible; you will find that there are many other opportunities out there waiting for you.

NOTEWORTHY SAYS:

- Educating your employers may be your greatest accomplishment
- Being in a bad job is like being in a bad relationship
- Today, people can have an average of seven or more jobs in a lifetime
- Most jobs—good jobs—are not advertised
- Pressure makes diamonds
- Consider the hospitality industry; it is full of opportunities

⊚ **12** ⊚

JOBS IN THE TWENTY-FIRST CENTURY

The landscape of the job market has changed dramatically in the 90s and it will continue to change as we enter the twenty-first century. Full-time, permanent jobs are becoming a thing of the past as we move toward more contract and fee-for-service arrangements with employers. Before, we had one primary, continuous consumer of our services, which was our boss. Now, we are looking at the prospect of providing services for many different customers or employers for varying lengths of time.

Currently, the largest single private employer in North America is a supplier of temporary services. This is indicative of the trend away from full-time, permanent jobs to fee-for-service arrangements. How do we respond to this changing job market and still find work that we love to do? To get some ideas, let's consider the following story of a family faced with changing employment trends and see how they were able to cope with those changes.

The Animal Kingdom Speaks

Long ago, before mankind and technology ruled the world, the animals in the forest had their own economic system, not unlike the one we humans use today. One of the more prominent animals in the forest and a contributor to that economy was the bear. Deep in the forest lived a family of bears that consisted of Mr. Bear, his wife, Mrs. Bear, and their teenage son, Junior Bear. As a progressive nuclear family, both parents had jobs at which they worked very hard while Junior went to school in the forest.

Mr. Lion, who lived on the edge of the forest, was pretty much in charge of things. However, because of his size, Mr. Bear had always occupied the number two spot in the food chain. It was a good position to be in because he didn't have the pressure of being responsible for the forest, while he maintained a considerable level of status.

Things went along happily, season after season, with Mr. Lion in charge and Mr. Bear in the number two position in the forest hierarchy. One day Mr. Lion came to visit Mr. Bear unexpectedly. As Mrs. Bear and Junior were out working and going to school, it happened that he caught Mr. Bear alone in the cave that day. Mr. Lion entered the cave and pulled up a chair at the Bear's table. He stretched his big paws out on top of the table as he sat back confidently and began to deliver his message.

"Mr. Bear, because we've had three harsh winters in a row, the economy of the forest has begun to suffer. Things are bad in my realm and I'm going to have to do some "restructuring," Mr. Lion said.

"What does that mean, restructuring?" Asked Mr. Bear.

"It means that the forest is in a recession and I need to reduce overhead from the top down," replied Mr. Lion.

"We've had hard winters before and we've always managed to come out on top, you in the number one position and myself in the number two position," said Mr. Bear.

"Things are different this time, Mr. Bear, I'm going to have to consolidate the management of the forest and I will no longer be needing anyone to occupy the number two position. I am revoking your hunting license."

"But Mr. Lion, I've always been number two in the forest. What else will I do if I can't hunt?"

"You could try working with the wolves at the other end of the forest, or you might consider moving to another area that may present more opportunities for yourself, Mrs. Bear and Junior."

"The wolves are scavengers! That would be the worst, and we can't move from our cave because of the job Mrs. Bear has here in the forest," Mr. Bear replied.

"I hate to give you the bad news all at once. I was hoping to tell each of you at different times, but now that I'm here, I might as well save a trip and let you give Mrs. Bear the news yourself. I've got to trim the fat somewhere, and unfortunately the buck stops here at your cave. You're both let go!" explained Mr. Lion.

Mr. Bear was at a loss at how to respond to this news. Finally he said plaintively, "We've been with you all our working life, I don't know what Mrs. Bear, Junior and I will do."

"Talk it over with the family and see what you can come up with. I'm sorry I can't do any more for you. I've got to get back to my hunting and I have a forest to run, so good luck and good-bye."

Mr. Lion got up and slowly walked out of the cave and into the forest without looking back. Mr. Bear was so shocked that he didn't even get up as Mr. Lion left. What on earth would he tell Mrs. Bear and Junior? True, he was a little grey in the fur around his mouth, but he still had some good employable years ahead of him. Working with the wolves would be far below his dignity. He was a proud hunter, not a scavenger; and he certainly wasn't about to give up the cozy cave he and Mrs. Bear had called home for all these years.

As the misery generated by the news was spiralling around him, Mrs. Bear and Junior entered the cave and found Mr. Bear sitting there in a despondent state.

"What's wrong, Dad?" asked Junior.

"Your father's probably just had a bad day in the forest; come and help me prepare the nuts and berries for dinner," said Mrs. Bear.

"It's all right; Junior, you're right. Something is wrong. Both of you had better come in here and let me tell you what's happened."

Mrs. Bear and Junior sat down at the table, and Mr. Bear presented the story of what had happened that day and what Mr. Lion had told him.

Junior reacted bravely to the news, and said, "I've almost finished school and I can go out and get a job. What's the big deal anyway, Dad?"

" We don't have many nuts and berries stored up and winter is coming and you need experience to get a job. That's the big deal!" Mr. Bear growled back at Junior.

Being more composed than Mr. Bear, Mrs. Bear calmly suggested, "Let's not let a little change in the labour market send us into a tizzy. We can come up with something; after all we are the Bears, the number two family in the forest!"

Mrs. Bear's resilience seemed to put a whole new spin on the situation, and the Bears started brainstorming. They tapped into the creative process and began building one idea on the next until they developed a plan. Junior would be finishing school soon, and although it would be too basic for Mr. Bear to work with the wolves, Junior could go and apprentice with them for a few seasons and learn a trade. No Bear had ever been in the scavenging trade before, but, as Mrs. Bear pointed out, in a challenging economy they would have to reexamine the way they thought about jobs. Besides, the crosscultural experience would be good for Junior and he would be earning a living while he was training.

Both Mr. and Mrs. Bear had built up a lot of contacts with the other animals in the forest during their many seasons of hunting. Although Mr. Bear tried to take credit for it, Mrs. Bear came up with an idea to become distributors of honey to all the animals in the forest. Just about every one they knew was a potential customer; even Mr. Lion liked a bit of honey every now and again. Mrs. Bear could work part-time helping the Beavers up at the dam and when the business developed, she could go full-time on the honey venture. All Mr. Bear had to do was to negotiate a deal with the Bees without getting stung too badly.

Everyone felt a lot better now that they had a plan in place. The more they thought about it, the better it looked. In fact, hunting was a bit of a messy job; and if things worked out the way they were hoping, the honey business could be a very good thing indeed.

The next day Mrs. Bear went out and immediately began networking with all her potential new customers for honey. The more she talked to the other animals about the honey, the more interest was generated in her product. Mr. Bear went down to try to make a deal with the Bees to distribute their honey. It turned out that the Bees were actually looking for new markets for their product and were very impressed with the number of contacts the Bears had. Consequently, Mr. Bear made a good deal and didn't get stung at all.

The business built slowly at first, but as time went by, things began to go quite well with their new venture. In fact, after a while they both agreed that the change in their occupation was the best thing that happened in their working lives. Not only did they have the same freedom they did with hunting, this business had great tax write-offs because they worked out of their cave.

It turned out that despite this change in the economy, Junior became a winner as well. Although he didn't go on to Bear University, he ended up doing better than most of its graduates; he learned practical, job-related skills. He became very good at scavenging, and actually came up with some new ideas and approaches to the old profession that made him very successful in his job. Later, when Mr. Bear retired, he wanted to give the business to Junior, but Junior was doing so well on his own, he didn't want it. Mr. and Mrs. Bear ended up selling the business to the foxes at a nice profit and retired comfortably; and they all lived happily ever after.

The Moral of the Story

The moral of the story is that in changing economies like the one the Bears went through and the one we are experiencing now, we must remain flexible and adaptable if we are to succeed. The key to working in today's economy is in having *entrepreneurial spirit.* We are going to have to start thinking in terms of ways to generate income as opposed to getting jobs. If you do work for someone else it comes back to running an industry within an industry as though it were your own. This way you will not be expendable.

To survive in the job market today, you need to have something people want and are willing to pay for. While you are working for others and learning about a business, where possible, do your best to develop skills in areas that will be portable to other jobs within your industry as well as other industries. If you have developed transferable skills, you now have developed skills that you can contract out to other organizations that may require your services.

As trends continue toward this type of contracting as opposed to old-time, permanent employment, we should, if we have a steady job, start storing those nuts and berries away before winter comes. Let's learn as much as we can and develop as many contacts as possible while we are under the protection of a regular paycheck. Does this sound disloyal? Does it seem like we are more interested in advancing ourselves than our employers? Of course not! Remember the formula; do something to advance the organization, but make sure you are doing something that will advance you. It is an exchange that any good employer *expects* and *respects*.

In this changing job market, you must think ahead. Is your job likely to be phased out when times get tough? Will your job be eliminated entirely by changes due to technology? We saw what happened to Mr. and Mrs. Bear. Not everyone is ready to go out and start their own business, but just like Mrs. Bear did, we might be able to come up with an area that we can develop on the side until we are ready.

Another way to enhance job creation is to take a step beyond gaining recognition in your job and begin to raise your profile in your industry. One way to do this is by becoming active in professional associations of which your organization may be a member. This is a great way to build up a lot of contacts within your industry and in other industries. These contacts can develop into valuable job leads or potential customers for future ventures, just like they did for the Bears.

Mr. Bear & the Bees

Contacts, Contacts, Contacts

Just like the Bears, you can never have too many contacts. In the 80s, it was *what* you knew that counted. In the 90s, it is *who* you know that counts. For the 21st century, things will be so tough, it may be *who you are related to* that counts! As soon as I realized this, I ran out and hired a couple of genetic research scientists. I commissioned them to find a link between myself and England's Royal Family. After an exhaustive search, it was revealed that I wasn't even related to the Queen's butler. Nice try! Forget about who you might be related to, let's focus on who you know and who you can get to know.

Training Versus Education in the 21st Century

One way to getting a better job is by increasing your level of marketable skills. In some cases, this can be done by going to school. In the modern world, not all of us have the luxury of attending university to become doctors and lawyers. Many of us will be forced to make a choice between education and training, just like Junior Bear was. Unless you are independently wealthy or have relatives who are, I suggest you take practical training over education. Education is a great thing but we need to eat. Get the training that will get you the job first, then get an education. In the meantime, I will give you a "quickie" degree consisting of four points that you need to learn to be successful (in the following order):

> 1. **LEARN how to *look* good.** Refer to Chapter Five, "Image Building," and remember, we are judged by how we look. This is not to say that we all have to look like models and movie stars to get ahead. However, we must always be "presentable plus."

The presentable part means that you can't go around with the poppy seeds from that bagel you had for lunch sticking between your teeth. Don't laugh, this is one of the more common grooming deficiencies. There are others. We've all been in one of those meetings where the person we are meeting with had those wacky hairs irreverently sticking out of their nose. How can people expect to be taken seriously by potential employers and customers if they can't even deal with personal grooming issues?

Now you think I'm being cruel. Forget it! It's a cruel world out there. No matter which way you want to slice the salami, personal appearance counts for a great deal. As politically correct as we have become, studies of personnel hiring trends show that attractive people are usually selected for jobs over less attractive applicants for the same job. Attractive people are treated differently in professional situations as well as in social situations.

I can remember being in situations where I was dressed very casually and perhaps had not shaved that day. The way I was treated in the same situation when I had a nice suit on was quite different. We've all experienced different versions of this discrimination. I am not saying that it is good, but it is a fact of life and part of human nature. All of us are beautiful people inside, but it takes time for people to get to know us well enough to find that out. In an age where time has become so precious, who can afford to? Let's face the issue and address it accordingly by being *presentable plus.*

The "plus" part of *presentable plus* is that little something extra that shows that we take pride in our appearance. That shine on your shoes that's a little brighter. Or investing in a colourful new tie. Or arranging that haircut a week or so earlier instead of trying to save a couple of bucks and waiting until people ask you what happened to your hair.

2.   **LEARN how to** *speak* **articulately.** We are judged by what we say; remember the Chapter Four, "Power to the Communicators," where we discussed behavioral imprints. Not only are we judged by what we say, but by how we *sound*. Continue to expand your vocabulary, use correct grammar and learn how to speak clearly and confidently. Use your voice as a tool to punctuate your communication so you sound like you know what you are talking about, even if you don't! The information is only one part of the communication, the rest is in the *delivery.*

When Dan Rather reads the nightly news to us do you think he has researched every story to determine how accurate it is? Of course not. Does he *sound* like he believes what he is saying? Of course he does! No matter how good of a communicator you are, you can always work on improving your delivery. A powerful delivery will go a long way to getting your message across.

    3. **LEARN how to *negotiate*.** Negotiation is a key area to develop if you want to be successful in any job. Although some people are natural negotiators, it is a skill that anyone can learn and develop through practise. It can be utilized in many areas of both our professional and personal lives. In fact, at some levels, negotiation is more than a skill, it is an art form. It has been said that he who masters the art of negotiation is the master of his world. (Remember Ned in Chapter Nine, "Climbing the Mountain.")

Although it may sound complicated, all of us began practising the art of negotiation at a very early age. In its crudest form, it began when we cried when we didn't get what we wanted. To simplify the process, let us say that negotiation is a matter of getting more of what you want more often.

How many times have we seen someone receive better pay or work under superior conditions, not because they did a better job than someone else, but because they were good negotiators? As we get closer to the prospect of working in a fee-for-service and contract environment, good negotiating skills will become a matter of survival. *Learn to negotiate.*

    4. **LEARN how to *write* effectively.** Be able to express yourself clearly in writing. The way you look and the way you sound will be the two most important things required to get a job. The way you write may be one of the things that gets you a promotion. Advanced skills in business correspondence, proposal writing and presentation development are worth a lot of money to an employer. Study and learn as

much as you can about them. These skills will also be worth a lot of money to you if you start doing contract work or go on to develop your own business.

My four-point "quickie" degree may seem like an over-simplification and may offend those involved in *higher* education. However, if you focus on these four things and learn how to do them effectively, you may be able to defer the *other* degree until you can afford that luxury. I remember joking with my friends in education, that when I got my book published and received my advance, I would be able to afford to enroll in that writing course I always wanted to take. Learn by doing. Skills first, education second.

Hybrids

Specialization was important for many jobs in the last twenty years or so. Today, the ability to serve different functions is what is in demand. Employers no longer have or want the infrastructure that is built on many specialists. Employers today want versatile people who can wear many hats.

In my years in the business world, historically there was a division between accounting/administrative types and marketing/PR types. They seem to mix (or not mix) like oil and water. During my time as a working musician, I recall a similar polarization between artists and business people that manifested itself in a deep distrust of one another. In my cumulative working experience, my observation has been that the most successful people in any field have been the ones with skills and talents in more than one area. The Hybrids—people who were not only creative, but could effectively sell their creations. Not only could they create a product, they could develop it in a business context. They were sales people who understood administration, accounting people who could relate to the sales process. They were the real winners. To tackle this dynamic job market, we must be flexible like the hybrids. We must be prepared to develop skills in more than one area. So keep an open mind to different work streams and become as adaptable as possible.

Never Stop Selling

As jobs become harder to find in the twenty-first century, we will have to become better than ever at selling. Although we call it marketing today, it is selling. If you feel better and more genteel by referring to it as marketing, go right ahead, but it's still selling, selling, selling! This is the most important single ingredient in our recipe for finding a job and succeeding in a job. Going back to what was discussed about image building and behavioral imprints, it all comes down to selling. Selling the most important product—yourself! As the market shifts towards fee-for-service, the one who is able to present, or sell, her product the best is the one most likely to get the job. As employees working for others, we are selling ourselves to our employers constantly.

All of us, in one way or another, are selling all the time. Remember the last time you told your mother-in-law you loved her meat loaf? Whether we realize it or not, we are selling all the time. Let's accept it. Better yet, let's embrace it and develop our selling skills to the highest level we can. I'm not going to go into how to sell because there are already a gazillion good books that you can read to help you in that area. If you are already selling, keep selling! If you don't relate to selling, get some of the many books on the subject and start selling. If the Bears can do it, anyone can!!

NOTEWORTHY SAYS:

- Adaptability and flexibility will be required to conquer changing job markets

- Try to develop an entrepreneurial spirit

- Heighten your personal profile through industry and professional associations

- Choose training before education

- Develop skills in the art of negotiation

- Never stop selling

❧ 13 ❧

YOU ARE WHAT YOU DO

Your Social Status and Your Job

When meeting new people in any social situation, what is the first meaningful question that you are sure to be asked? You guessed it! "What do you do for a living?" Why is this of so much interest to people you have never met before? Because the kind of job you have is a big qualifier as to who you are. Your job relates to your personal power base, your income level, even how interesting you might be, as perceived by others. It would be nice to think that who we are under the surface is really what counts and that the kind of job we do is only secondary to our true essence. In this material world, it seems that what people are interested in the most about us is what we *do* for a living.

And let's admit it, so are we. How many times have we embellished our employment situation to make it sound more important or more interesting than it really is? Think of all those occasions in public settings when you were asked what you did for a living and you were compelled to stretch the truth, even a little bit. What about the times you wanted to prefabricate that you were in some exciting profession or in a lofty position of importance? When you wished you could answer that question by saying, "I'm with the CIA," or "I'm a global venture capitalist, returning from a project in Asia," or something equally impressive.

Why would levelheaded, mature individuals like us feel compelled to misrepresent ourselves when asked such a simple, harmless question? Because there is nothing simple or harmless about that question at all. This is the first question with teeth that we will encounter in any introductory social situation. Answering this question is as bad as filling out a credit application or having a blood test. In fact, this issue has become so sensitive that we have developed all sorts of catch phrases and socially elevating terminology to describe one's employment situation as favourably as possible.

For instance, we no longer have a mailman, we now have a postal service technician. Taxi drivers have been replaced by tourism transport operators. You can't even be a panhandler any more because you are now a socially displaced entrepreneur! Because of the tremendous pressure exerted by society on us to amount to something, to be somebody, our level of employment is the single most important social qualifier there is.

To get an idea of how deeply the need to be successful is in our society, we only have to look at the significance that is placed on one of the most important material possessions that can be acquired (and the second most important social qualifier) —the automobile! Although people are hard-pressed to come out and ask you what kind of car you drive, this is of critical interest to most. A car, just like a job seems to define who we are!

In order to satiate this need to identify us with our vehicles, and to get more mileage out of this perversion, I've come up with an interesting idea. I am trying to promote the development of a chain of nightclubs and restaurants that will enable the patrons to park directly on the dance floor or between the dining tables. This way, people will be able to attach themselves directly to their status symbols!!

At present, the closest thing we have to this is valet parking. But my idea is much better, because with valet parking, people only see you with your vehicle for a few seconds when you are getting in or out of it. With my system, you will be able to impress people for the entire evening (with the possible exception of having to leave your vehicle to go to the washroom once or twice). And here's an example of an original, unorthodox idea as well!

Okay, I'll admit it, the idea is not one hundred percent original. The part about parking on the dance floor is original. The idea of parking between the tables at the restaurant is a modification of what was done in some restaurants in the fifties where food was served directly to your car. These venues were popular because not only could you have your favourite meal, you could preempt social qualifying by flaunting your status symbols directly at one another. My idea may be farfetched, but it is a clear illustration of the intensity of social qualifying. (And if someone does something with my idea, I want royalties.)

At all levels of the food chain, we are susceptible to being socially qualified. When I have that first dinner date with a new acquaintance, I'm always suspicious that when she excuses herself to use the powder room, she's actually on the phone running a Dunn & Bradstreet check on me! Fortunately (for now) we don't have to carry copies of our resumés and career accomplishments with us wherever we go, but that ever-present question is always lurking in the wings for us. Let's be prepared to answer it intelligently and be able to back it up with something substantial as well.

Although it is much more prevalent today, the issue of "you are what you do" is certainly nothing new. I can remember back to the days of my career as a musician. When I was performing in a popular nightclub, I had the ultimate level of prestige with the customers, particularly the females. Everyone wanted to be part of the band in some way, to hang out with you, to date the musicians. However, when I came back to the same nightclub on a night off and was not part of the scene, people would not give me the time of day! The same nightclub, the same patrons. I was the same person as I was the night before, but now I had an entirely different level of social status. I am sure that most of us have had a version of this experience.

To get a better view of how your job relates to your social status, just turn to the timeless forum where social qualifying is more intense than anywhere else … in the "mating game." In the past, qualities such as having a good sense of humour, being sensitive or having a pleasant personality had importance. Today, the first and foremost thing on a potential mate's mind is "I want to meet someone with a good job!"

What unattached people are looking for in other unattached individuals is always an excellent barometer of prevailing social conditions. After all, these people are on the forefront of social interaction. They know exactly what they are looking for in others and they have the freedom to settle for nothing less. As a single person, if you think that what you do for a living is not important to people, just pick up any newspaper and take a look in the personal classified section where people "shop" to meet other people. The majority of the people placing the ads are looking for things like a nonsmoking individual with *secure employment,* or an athletic *professional* person, or an outgoing *successful* person etc.

The Schmuck Versus the Medical Student

Again, this is nothing new. I remember experiencing it in the good old dating days as a young man in my twenties. My friend and I used to visit the various haunts of single people where the mating game was in full swing on a Friday or Saturday night. When we began to chat with the young women and that inevitable question about "what we did" popped up, I was always amazed at the outcome.

My reply of "I play in a band" was usually good for a favourable response. However, when my friend began to tell the women that he was a medical student, it was all over. They went nuts about this! The guy didn't look any different than he had twenty minutes earlier when we arrived at the place, and I'm sure he hadn't grown any taller since we had been there! Although I was tempted to claim that I was a brain surgeon on many subsequent occasions, I instead decided to stop going to those places with him.

To this day, this issue is still critical for single people. Let's face it, your ability to attract someone into a relationship can be directly related to your level of employment. For purists and idealists this will be hard to take, but the sooner we accept society's concern with our position in the food chain, the sooner we can get on with learning to love our job and start having fun!

The saving grace to this prevailing social infatuation is that it can provide us with one of the most powerful motivators for achieving career bliss. It is an excellent motivator for those of us who are not so strongly self-motivated. Why not try to take our career right over the top? The whole world is behind us on this one.

NOTEWORTHY SAYS:

- Your level of employment is the biggest single social qualifier

- Be realistic—where we are in the food chain counts!

- Be creative; embellish your level of employment— but don't lie!

- We can use social pressure as a motivator to make our job better

∞ **14** ∞

KEEP ON LOVING YOUR JOB

Revisiting Your Commitment

We've broken the bonds of occupational slavery and got our job working for us instead of us working for our job. Our accomplishments are being driven by our need to excel as individuals, not just as employees. We have taken ownership of our job, and now our commitment to our work is a labour of love. Where do we go from here?

Now that we are closer to attaining career bliss, the challenge has just begun. We have climbed the mountain just like Ned (Chapter Nine), but to keep loving your job is to climb a mountain that has no summit or peak. Your ascent to success is a journey that will continue throughout your career and perhaps your entire lifetime.

Staying in love with your work is similar to maintaining your love for another person. You have to work at and nurture that relationship for as long as you continue to participate in it. Your love for your work may be challenged over time, and confirmation will be required again and again. But working at the relationship is what love is really all about, isn't it?

Honesty

In order to keep loving our job, we must continually evaluate ourselves and assess our progress. Just as we expect honesty in a personal relationship, we must be honest with ourselves about our relationship with our work. In our assessment we are going to have to be as objective as possible and ask ourselves some of the following questions:

- ❑ Have we obtained the goals we set for ourselves?
- ❑ Were these goals achieved within the desired time frame?
- ❑ If we have fallen short of our original goal, were we realistic in setting that goal?
- ❑ Could we have done more to reach our goals?
- ❑ If we could have done more, why didn't we?

To get an accurate reading on where we are in our career at any given time, we will be required to be brutally honest with ourselves when we answer these questions.

Our greatest obstacle to being honest will be our human tendency toward rationalization. Excuses like: I don't think I have the ambition, or I didn't have the opportunity, or my spouse wouldn't like it, or I might get hit by a bus tomorrow so why bother, etc., come from an endless list that we love to use. It's certainly a lot easier to refer to our catalogue of excuses and blame the prevailing state of affairs on everything and everyone but ourselves.

The real struggle is in facing ourselves and admitting that we may have let ourselves down somewhere along the way. Our salvation is that as soon as we accept our mistakes, that struggle is over and we can continue our climb with renewed vision.

Cycles

Just about everything around us runs in some kind of a cycle. Business cycles, weather cycles, life cycles, over and over in natural perpetuation. How we feel about our job at any given time is part of yet another cycle. In spite of what some motivational gurus may tell us, we simply cannot be 100 percent, over-the-top effective, twenty-four hours a day! It is not possible. Not only is it impossible, it is not natural.

Each of us has a natural cycle of emotional ups and downs that is part of normal day-to-day living. It is very important to take into account where we are in our cycle and plan our activities accordingly (see chart on page 163). Although we cannot control the cycle, we can have some influence over how sustained any one stage of the cycle is. Obviously, we want to spend more time sustaining the ascending and peak stages than the descending stages.

To minimize your time in a low point of the cycle, try to gain some objectivity (see Chapter Eight, "Erogenous Zones"). Remember to consider not only your weaknesses, but your strengths as well. Give yourself credit for your accomplishments and try to get jump-started by getting back in touch with the momentum you generated with those accomplishments.

If you continue having difficulty getting out of a low point, I recommend adjusting your workload to involve yourself with other people as much as possible. If you are trying to get back on the ascending side of your cycle, the last thing you want to do is to spend time alone amongst your paperwork, as seductive as it may sound. Our coworkers and customers are an excellent source of objectivity and can provide a valuable point of reference. It may seem basic, but as soon as we get some exposure to other peoples' expectations of themselves, we will quickly see that we are a lot better off than we originally thought we were.

OUR EMOTIONAL CYCLE

Recommended activities for different stages of the cycle:

Presentations, influential interpersonal activities

PEAK

Development of creative projects

Focus on originality

Analysis, modifications of existing
systems and procedures

ASCENDING

DESCENDING

Planning, product development

Paper work, technical reading

LOW

"Grunt" work

Don't Give Up

To achieve all the objectives presented in this book is not an overnight process. Like anything worth achieving, it will take time and effort to study and practise the information before you can receive all the potential benefits. Don't be discouraged if your career does not turn around one hundred and eighty degrees by the time you finish reading this book. *Anyone who tells you they became successful overnight is either an heir or an idiot!* Take the one idea most relevant to your situation and apply it. Then build on that success by trying another idea. If you try to do too much, too fast, you won't be happy with the results and you may question the methods before you give them a chance to work for you.

Not all of the information may be applicable to the current stage of your career. However, as your career develops—hopefully due in part to what we have discussed—refer back to the book and you will most likely find something you can use at that time.

Busy Hands are Happy Hands

No matter how slowly you may think you are progressing, keep working at it! *Thinking* about what to do to improve things or *talking* about how to make things better have never produced the results that *doing something about it* has! As long as we are actively pursuing ways to love our job and have more fun with our career, we are winning the battle.

If we can sustain those pursuits, we will win the war! If you feel you are not quite ready to make a change yet and you need more ideas to get you started, I suggest reading *What Color Is Your Parachute?* by Richard Bolles.

Whatever you do, never give up. Never stop believing there is a better way to work and earn a living. Tomorrow you can become more than you are today. And if someone ever tells you that you can't succeed at something, listen carefully to what they say. When you spend the rest of your life proving how wrong they were, you want to be able to thank them for their words of encouragement.

Growing Old Together

If you can master the skills discussed here and learn to love your job, you will have found the way to control your career destiny. Because all employers love employees who love their jobs, you will be in a position to increase your earning potential as well as your job security. If the skills can help you start your own business or to begin contracting your services directly to customers, even greater opportunities await you.

Best of all, you won't have to worry about what is going to happen next in your career. You will be in charge of it! Most people will be counting the days until they reach retirement age, dreaming of each working year passing over them like sheep in their sleep. *You* will be banging the door down to get in to work every day. You will have the potential to become so successful at what you do, when you get too old to work, they'll have to pry you away from your desk kicking and screaming (at the age of about 101).

Whistle While You Work

Wouldn't you love to be the one that the crotchety old barnacles at work are talking about when they muse to one another during their coffee break? You will be the person about whom they wonder, "What are they so bloody happy about?" What a triumph it will be to step over the nay-sayers as we come into our own. Misery loves company and it will try to lure you in—especially you—because you're going to have so much going for you. Reject it, deny it, and resist it. Stick to the master plan and keep refining your skills and increasing your knowledge.

If the din of negativity around you begins to distract you, take a lesson from the seven dwarves and whistle while you work! The doom-and-gloomers will eventually give up on you because the positive momentum you create will start to affect even them. Keep it up!

Do the Best With What You Have

I was back home with a few days off from a tour of the Eastern U.S. As a musician, I liked to hang out with some of the seedier elements of society, as the role dictates. We were playing cards late into the wee hours of the morning and drinking a bit, I'm sure. What else we were doing I can't remember and if I could, I certainly wouldn't admit to it on paper. The last thing I recall was being dealt three aces. The next thing I knew, I was laying in the hospital in intensive care with tubes sticking out of me everywhere, drifting in and out of consciousness.

Each time I gained consciousness, I screamed with pain. Whether it was the delirium or the Demoral, I remember a nurse coming over and saying, "Keep it down! You're not the only one dying in here!" Then one of the orderlies explained to me that I was in the "snake pit," where some customers came out all right and others didn't.

This information was not that reassuring, and when I looked down at the arm that was most important to my guitar playing and saw my hand as a mess of pulp in a plaster cast red with blood, I really started wailing!

The next event I recall was being awakened by this large man with a surgical mask covering most of his face. In tones muffled by his mask he said, "I'm going to have to set your wrist and we can't give you anaesthetic because of your other injuries, so this is going to hurt a bit."

As the powerful hands of this inquisitioner gripped my tender, broken wing and began twisting, I wouldn't have been surprised if some of my old friends up at the mine heard me scream. The next thing I remember was laying quietly with my arm throbbing in unison with the rest of my body. I was in a room with three other guys in a ward within the hospital.

I finally got the story from two policemen and someone from the insurance company who came to ask me where I had been prior to the accident. I honestly remember nothing but three aces followed by an avalanche of pain, and that's exactly what I told them.

I was told that I drove off the road on a hairpin turn on a lonely stretch of the Trans-Canada highway. Apparently, the car began to roll as it left the road at high speed and I was thrown out of the car (I wasn't wearing a seat belt). I must have put my hand out to break my fall and severely broke my wrist instead. The car then rolled on top of me and crushed my chest.

Another driver eventually came along and saw the car upside down with me under it and called for help. I was taken by ambulance to the hospital and pieced back together like a jigsaw puzzle. I would remain there for many weeks during my recovery. There were to be three operations and extensive therapy to follow for that battered, guitar-playing wrist. This was all pretty scary because, prior to this happening, I was at the height of my technical prowess musically, some say at the point where I had the most "fire" in my playing.

I wish I could tell you that I met God or I had an out-of-body experience, but I can't. All I can tell you is that it was very frightening and I had a lot of pain. However, the day I limped out of there, I had a major realization. I realized how lucky I was to be alive and every day I lived after that was free time, a bonus.

Most people, including the doctors, were pretty surprised that I was able to play the guitar again. In fact, the majority of my career as a musician took place after the accident. There were many technical things that I was not capable of after I was injured, and I would never have the physical ability to become a guitar virtuoso, but I was determined to see how far I could go with what I had.

Never Stop Dreaming

Although most of the people I knew thought I was crazy to struggle away for years trying to be a musician, I took it as far as I could before I had to break down and get a "real" job. When my friends all had steady jobs and homes and families, I was out there slogging away in smoky night clubs trying to make an artistic "difference."

In the end, it wasn't my wrist as much as the lifestyle that made me retire. Rather than give up my dream of becoming successful, I had to change it to reflect reality. And to quote Robert James Waller from his book, *The Bridges of Madison County:* "Although most of my dreams never came true, I'm still glad I had them." After I made the decision to stop playing professionally, I would never ask myself, "I wonder what would have happened if I'd kept going?" When I made that decision, I was facing another reality. Until then,

I had only wanted to be a musician. I never wanted to grow up, let alone get a "real" job! I had minimal formal education and supposedly limited transferable skills. I faced the challenge of remaining creative and learning how to love a different kind of job. How would I survive in the "real" world of work? Obviously, I did. And in the hope that it will make your way easier, it has been my pleasure to share with you some of the things that I have learned in *my* struggle to love working. If I could do it, I'll bet you can too, so have fun, fall in love ... and get paid to do it!

ORDER FORM

Qty.	Title	Ccanada	U.S.	Australia	Total
	Have Fun, Fall in Love...	$16.95	$14.95	$19.95	
				Subtotal	
	Shipping and Handling (add $3.00 for one book, $1.00 for each additional book)				
	Canadian residents add 7% GST; Washington residents only, add 8.2% sales sax				
				Total Enclosed	

Payment Method: Please Check One:

❏   Cheque (Payable to Peanut Butter Publishing)

❏   Postal money order

❏   **Credit Card Orders:**
Expiration Date: _____/_____
Card #: _____
Name on Card: _____
Signature : _____

❏   **FAX Orders:**
1-604-688-0132. Fill out
the order blank and fax.

❏   **e mail Orders:**
pnutpub@aol.com

❏   **Internet Orders:**
http://www.pbpublishing.com

❏   [MasterCard]   ❏   [VISA]

Please send to:

NAME _____

ADDRESS _____

CITY _____

PROVINCE/STATE _____ POSTAL/ZIP CODE _____

DAYTIME PHONE _____

PEANUT BUTTER PUBLISHING

Suite 230, 1333 Johnston Street • Pier 32, Granville Island
Vancouver, B.C. V6H 3R9

226 2nd Avenue West • Seattle, WA 98119

Quantity discounts are available.
For more information, call 604-688-0320
Thank you for your order!